Yes, You *Can* Stay Sober

If you are ready—or know someone who's ready—to achieve and maintain sobriety, here's an approach that will work. Unlike other books on recovery, The Staying Sober Handbook is unique because it...

- ...stands upon a bedrock of personal experience plus a broad base of the most advanced findings in science, technology, and clinical practice.

- ...provides a wealth of physical, emotional, mental & spiritual techniques and resources for all involved: addict, family, friends and clinicians.

- ...is built on a new paradigm in addiction treatment that recognizes addiction as a chronic, progressive brain condition—a persistent medical ailment that can be managed.

- ...contains all 24 sobriety tools, assembled over nine years of real-life wisdom and experience from hundreds of people and thousands of hours of hard work, fine-tuning, and refinement.

- ...presents the unique S.O.B.E.R. Action Plan, a step-by-step self-designed program you can rely on to stay on track and is free of guilt-producing rules and restrictions.

- ...delivers information, action steps, workable exercises, and, most importantly, genuine experience-based encouragement to anyone involved in any phase of addiction and recovery.

Written by a therapist who has himself navigated the path through addiction and into long-term recovery, *Staying Sober* is an intuitively conceived and brilliantly executed presentation.

If you're thinking about getting sober, this book will show you that you *can* do it and how to get there. If you're sober and want to strengthen your resources for staying that way, this will provide the support you need. If you're a family member or loved one of someone suffering from addiction, your life is affected, too—big time—and this book can restore stability and sanity. And if you are a clinician or therapist, you will find solid ideas for amplifying the effectiveness of your practice with addicts.

Are you ready?

About the Author

Howard Goodman, MA, LMFT is a licensed psychotherapist, specializing in the treatment of addiction since 2006. Over the last ten years Howard has treated individuals in hospitals, inpatient, intensive outpatient, and sober living facilities as well as in his private practice. In recovery himself, Howard brings a personal sense  of urgency, empathy and purpose to help others achieve long-term sobriety, health, and wellness.

Howard maintains a private practice in Los Angeles where he treats individuals, couples, and families recovering from addiction. Goodman is a frequent blog contributor, public speaker, and CEU workshop presenter. For more information on Howard P. Goodman, please visit www.howardpgoodman.com

THE
STAYING
SOBER
HANDBOOK

THE
STAYING
SOBER
HANDBOOK

A STEP-BY-STEP GUIDE
TO LONG-TERM RECOVERY
FROM ADDICTION

HOWARD P. GOODMAN, MA, LMFT

Malibu, CA

Strandline Press
23823 Malibu Road, Suite #249
Malibu, CA 90265
(424) 781-7949
www.Strandlinepress.com

Printed in the United States of America

Publisher's Cataloguing-in-Publication Data

Names: Goodman, Howard P., author.

Title: The staying sober handbook : a step-by-step guide to long-term recovery from addiction / Howard P. Goodman.

Description: Malibu, CA : Strandline Press, [2016] | Includes bibliographical references and index.

Identifiers: ISBN: 978-0-9967449-0-4 | 978-0-9967449-1-1 | LCCN: 2015913805

Subjects: LCSH: Addicts--Rehabilitation--Handbooks, manuals, etc. | Alcoholics--Rehabilitation-- Handbooks, manuals, etc. | Drug addicts--Rehabilitation--Handbooks, manuals, etc. | Substance abuse--Relapse--Prevention--Handbooks, manuals, etc. | Alcoholism--Relapse --Prevention--Handbooks, manuals, etc. | Drug addiction--Relapse--Prevention--Handbooks, manuals, etc. | Recovering addicts--Handbooks, manuals, etc. | Recovering alcoholics-- Handbooks, manuals, etc. | LCGFT: Handbooks and manuals. | BISAC: SELF-HELP / Substance Abuse & Addictions / General | SELF-HELP / Substance Abuse & Addictions / Alcohol | SELF-HELP / Substance Abuse & Addictions / Drugs | SELF-HELP / Codependency | SELF-HELP / Adult Children of Substance Abusers | SELF-HELP / Compulsive Behavior / Sex & Pornography Addiction

Classification: LCC: HV4998 .G66 2016 | DDC: 362.29/186--dc23

Book Shepherd: Ellen Reid
Cover Design: Lewis Agrell
Interior Design: Ghislain Viau

To Aaron and Michael

Disclaimer

This book is presented solely for educational purposes. While best efforts have been used in preparing this book, the author and publisher make no representations or warranties of any kind and assume no liabilities of any kind with respect to the accuracy or completeness of the contents. This book is not meant to be used, nor should it be used, to diagnose or treat any medical condition. For diagnosis or treatment of any medical problem, consult your own physician or qualified health care professional. The publisher and author are not responsible for any damages or negative consequences from any treatment, action, application or preparation, to any person reading or following the information in this book. References are provided for informational purposes only and do not constitute endorsement of any websites or other sources. Readers should be aware that the websites and contact information listed in this book may change.

Contents

Acknowledgments   xv

Introduction   1

PART ONE

Staying Sober
Staying Sober and the Current State of Addiction Treatment

Chapter 1: You Can Stay Sober!   9

Chapter 2: Guiding Principles of Staying Sober   13

Chapter 3: The Medical Model of Addiction   17

Chapter 4: The Cycle of Addiction and How to Break It   21

PART TWO

Early Recovery
Learning the 24 Skills Needed to Shift from Addictive to Recovery-Based Thinking, Feeling, Behavior, and Activities

Chapter 5: Cognitive-Based Sobriety Skills   33

Skill # 1 CBT   39

Skill # 2 Affirmations   44

Skill # 3 Attitude of Gratitude   50

Skill # 4 Reading Daily Meditation   52

Skill # 5 Journaling   54

Chapter 6: Mindfulness-Based Sobriety Skills   57

Skill # 6 Mindfulness Meditation   57

Skill # 7 Visualization   64

Skill # 8 Mapping Triggers with Body Scan   67

Skill # 9 The Power of Prayer   70

Chapter 7: Sobriety-Centric Behaviors   77

Skill # 10 Boundary Setting   77

Skill # 11 Sober Home/Work/School   79

Skill # 12 Personal Appearance/Hygiene   82

Skill # 13 Self-Soothing Behaviors   84

Skill # 14 Healthy Diet and Nutrition   87

Chapter 8: Sobriety-Centric Activities   93

Skill # 15 Attend Support Group Meetings/AA   93

Skill # 16 Sober Support Network   98

Skill # 17 Sober FUN!   99

Skill # 18 Active Listening   102

Skill # 19 Assertive Communications   105

Skill # 20 Dealing with Resentments   109

Skill # 21 Making Amends   111

Skill # 22 Bookending   115

Skill # 23 Taking Contrary Actions   116

Skill # 24 Putting It Together with a SOBER Action Plan   119

PART THREE

Mid Recovery

*Integrating Individual Staying Sober Skills
into a Balanced, Sober Lifestyle*

Chapter 9: *Width* in Recovery—Measuring the Quality
of Sobriety   127

Chapter 10: Understanding the Spectrum of Sobriety (SOS)   131

Chapter 11: Using the SOS Checklist   135

Chapter 12: Creating a Day with the Staying Sober
Recovery Planner   137

PART FOUR

Long-Term Recovery
Growth, Development, and Personal Transformation

Chapter 13: Maintenance and Ongoing Growth   145

Chapter 14: *Depth* in Recovery—The Process of
Transformation   147

Chapter 15: Deepening Sobriety through Acts of Service   151

PART FIVE

Challenges in Recovery
*Getting Stuck in Recovery: How to Identify
Challenges and Overcome Them*

Chapter 16: Self-Defeating Behavior Patterns and
How to Overcome Them   159

Chapter 17: Incomplete Recovery   169

Chapter 18: Post-Acute Withdrawal Symptoms (PAWS)   179

Chapter 19: Overcoming PAWS with PRINTS   191

PART SIX

Guide to Family Healing
*Promoting Family Healing, Addressing Outstanding Issues,
and Creating New House Rules for Returning Loved Ones:
Addiction Is a Family Disease That Affects Everyone*

Chapter 20: The Addicted Family System   197

Chapter 21: Promoting Family Healing   203

Chapter 22: Codependence   205

Chapter 23: Codependence Self-Assessment   207

Chapter 24: Recovering from Codependence   211

Chapter 25: Setting Healthy Boundaries with
Those in Recovery   215

Chapter 26: House Rules and Family Safety Plan   221

Chapter 27: Ending the Blame Game   233

Chapter 28: Creating a Family Genogram   235

PART SEVEN

Clinician's Guide to Addiction Treatment

*Everything You Ever Wanted to Know about Addiction
Treatment, But Were Never Taught at School*

Chapter 29: Clinical Barriers to Treatment   243

Chapter 30: Clinical Ambivalence toward AA   249

Chapter 31: America's Love of "Wonder Drugs"   255

Chapter 32: Our Confused Drug Policies   259

Chapter 33: Assessing Your Views on Addiction   263

Chapter 34: Motivational Interviewing   267

Chapter 35: Guiding Principles of Motivational Interviewing   273

Chapter 36: The OARS Technique   279

The Road Ahead   287

Referrals and Resources   291

Suggested Reading   295

Bibliography   297

Index   305

Acknowledgments

Thank you, Greg Hannley, for giving me the opportunity to experiment, fine tune, and implement my approach to addiction treatment at your facilities. Your work and life inspire me on a daily basis to continue "living the dream."

I also want to thank Ellen Reid and her team. Her expertise, intuition, and leadership helped make this book possible.

Introduction

My road to recovery began with a pounding on my front door in the dead of night. It was 3 a.m. I got out of bed, unsteadily made my way down the stairs, and peered through the peephole. Standing on the other side were two men in suits. "Police," they identified themselves through the closed door. "We're here to ask your son a few questions."

"What?" I barked, opening the door. I had gone to bed drunk that night. I did not understand their request, nor was I in any mood to talk to them or anyone else. I refused to cooperate. I was ready to slam the door in their faces when I heard my wife call to me from the upstairs landing.

I apparently had been so loud and belligerent that I managed to wake up my wife and sons. They stared down at me in fear and disbelief from the second-floor landing. My wife managed to calm me down enough to reengage with the detectives.

They said they believed my son had been involved in a burglary. They reminded me that he was still on probation for a prior offense.

This gave them the right to show up, unannounced, at any time to question him and search his premises without a warrant.

Finally, I relented and permitted my son to meet with the detectives. It soon became obvious they were not strangers to one another. In fact, my son had apparently had a number of previous brushes with local law enforcement, of which I was not aware.

My anger and frustration over my son's drug use and criminal activity soon gave way to fear and dread for his freedom. He had been seen breaking into a neighbor's car and stealing money—a felony.

Ultimately my son was sentenced to three years in a juvenile correctional institution. The sheriff's department informed me that boys my son's age were often victimized by bigger, stronger inmates and that law enforcement would not be able to keep him safe in that setting.

I pleaded with the judge to allow him to serve his sentence at a facility where he could receive treatment rather than punishment for his addiction. The judge agreed, under the condition that it was a secure (read "locked down") facility.

I was given a month to find a facility that met these criteria. After scouring the western United States, I located one in Utah. At the sentencing hearing, the judge instructed me to get him into this facility within forty-eight hours; otherwise, a bench warrant would be issued for him and me. We walked out of the courthouse, climbed into my car, and headed for Utah.

It was late evening by the time we finally arrived at the treatment center. We were ordered to say our goodbyes. A moment later, I watched my son disappear behind a door and into the facility. I stood there, dumbfounded. How could this have happened? How did my son go from a fun-loving, football-playing, high school student to an incarcerated juvenile criminal? How had I lost control? Where was I to blame?

Feelings of guilt, shame, and remorse settled in beside me on the passenger seat as I set off back across the desert in the darkness. Past conversations with my son ran through my head. "What's the difference between you drinking every night and me smoking weed?" he would throw back in my face when we argued about his drug use.

"Plenty! For one thing, alcohol is legal—and for another, I am an adult who has his life together!" was my self-righteous, knee-jerk response. But tonight, alone in my car as I drove across the barren desert landscape, that answer sounded strangely hollow, self-serving, and untrue.

In my heart of hearts, I knew I had a drinking problem. But up until then I had clung to the delusion that I had my drinking under control. As long as it did not affect my work, I told myself, I did not really have a problem. And yet, I knew that all my previous attempts to cut back or quit drinking had been unsuccessful. The truth was, I could not stop drinking, even if I wanted to.

Suddenly, the idea of sitting in judgment of my son's substance abuse while rationalizing that mine was under control started to unravel. The hypocrisy of it all ripped away the delicately constructed fabric of elaborately woven lies, half-truths, and delusions I dressed myself in for years.

The naked truth was, my drinking had slowly, imperceptibly progressed from "taking the edge off after a hard day at work" to getting drunk every night. My life had devolved into a pattern of going to work, coming home, and drinking until I found myself alone, passed out on the couch around midnight.

This hit me like a fist to the gut. Disgusted, nauseated, I pulled off the road in front of a sign announcing I was in "The Valley of Fire." I threw open the car door and began retching uncontrollably. My stomach was empty. All that came up was the bitter taste of bile in the back of my throat and the still more bitter recognition that I was an alcoholic who had failed so thoroughly as a parent and father that I'd been forced to hand over the welfare of my son to strangers.

By the time I pulled into my driveway at home that morning, I had resolved that it was finally time for me to get sober. I'd had a moment of clarity in the hellish Valley of Fire. I promised myself it was time to change and get sober. I had made many similar promises, but this time I was sincerely determined to quit.

What I learned was that sincerity and determination are necessary to staying sober, but they are not sufficient. It would take another five years for me to learn exactly what to do, on a daily basis, to stay sober. In my case, that meant transforming my life. I entered individual therapy, and I began attending Alcoholics Anonymous (AA) meetings. My sobriety date is October 3, 2006.

I became so interested in the healing power of therapy and recovery that I eventually sold my business, and, at age forty-eight, I returned to school. I earned a master's in psychology and became a licensed psychotherapist, specializing in chemical dependency.

Since that time, I have spent thousands of hours working with people from virtually all ages, races, socioeconomic groups, cultures, and sexual/gender orientations to help them stay sober. Along the way, I identified 24 highly effective skills, practices, activities, tips, and techniques to implement a plan to stay sober and enjoy a drug-free lifestyle beyond one's wildest imaginings.

All 24 sobriety tools are in this book. They reflect nine years of real-life wisdom and experience from hundreds of people and thousands of hours of hard work, fine-tuning, and refinement. The bottom line is, when implemented as described, Staying Sober works!

An early insight in recovery that resonates more deeply with each passing year is, "The work does not end, but neither do the rewards." For me, that work is being of service to others. It is the most satisfying activity I know.

These noble principles notwithstanding, I must also confess that my motives are as selfish as they are selfless. My own recovery depends on being of service to others. It is perhaps the most important thing I do to stay sober on a daily basis. It is one of those counterintuitive ideas that is both spiritual as practical:

"We need to give away our recovery in order to keep it."

It is in that spirit, I offer this book.
Love,

Howard
Malibu, California, 2015

PART ONE

Staying Sober

*Staying Sober and the Current
State of Addiction Treatment*

Chapter 1: You Can Stay Sober!

Chapter 2: Guiding Principles of Staying Sober

Chapter 3: The Medical Model of Addiction

Chapter 4: The Cycle of Addiction and How to Break It

You Can Stay Sober!

You can stay sober. It is as simple as taking your daily medicine. Millions of people use the following approach to manage their recovery on a daily basis. You can too.

Staying Sober will teach you, step by step, how to create a new, drug-free way of being in the world. You will develop your own goals and objectives. You will set your own pace and learn how to create a new way of life beyond your wildest imaginings.

The only question is: *Are you ready?* Are you ready to free yourself from the fatal grip of addiction? Are you sick and tired of being sick and tired? And are you finally ready to end the downward spiral of crisis, negative consequences, and chaos? Do you want to create a sober lifestyle filled with happiness, meaning, purpose, and your own version of success?

My Promise to You

Here is my promise to you. I will guide you through the Staying Sober process. I will never ask you to do anything that countless others and I, myself, have not done. I will be at your side, teaching you skills, giving you exercises to practice, and providing you with helpful information, encouragement, personal stories, examples, and useful tips.

There are no time limits or finish lines. You get to take as much time as you need, and you can start over any time. I will *never* give up on you. I know this approach works. It has for me. It can for you. The only question is: *Are you ready?* If so, read on.

The Best Time *Ever* to Get Sober

There has never been a better time to get sober than today. We have learned more about the nature of addiction and effective ways to treat it in the past twenty-five years than in the previous 2,500!

Here are just some of the highlights:

- New PET (Positron-Emission Tomography) and fMRI (functional Magnetic Resonance Imaging) scanning technologies enable us to study the impact of addiction on the brain in real time.
- The creation of addiction medicine—a new medical specialty devoted specifically to help people recover from addiction.
- Breakthrough discoveries and research on the neurochemistry of addiction and the impact of drugs on brain structures and behavior.
- Comprehensive, long-term studies showing which types of therapy are most effective, as measured by treatment outcomes that promote long-term (twelve months or more) abstinence from drugs and alcohol.
- Increase in services. Nationwide, we have more treatment centers (more than 16,000) serving more individuals with more evidence-based treatment practices than ever before.

- Record levels of federal funding for addiction services, research, and education. The annual budget for the Substance Abuse and Mental Health Services Administration (SAMHSA) is now more than three billion dollars.

- Increased public awareness of addiction as a medical/mental health condition that requires treatment instead of a law enforcement issue requiring punishment.

- A new paradigm in addiction treatment, recovery management, is producing significantly better long-term outcomes.

It is helpful to remember that, prior to 1935, none of the above existed. Those addicts and alcoholics who were wealthy enough could check themselves into private hospitals or health spas—places to go "dry out." The rest of us tended to end up in psychiatric wards, hospital emergency rooms, jail, or the morgue. The fact that you are reading this page separates you from thirty-five million other Americans who are still in the fatal grip of their addiction.

Getting the Most from This Book

What are my chances of staying sober?

Quite good, based on my personal experience, clinical work with others in recovery, and the findings of SAMHSA's long-term outcome studies. To borrow a phrase from AA, "It works if you work it."

Staying Sober is not a magic bullet or quick fix. No such thing exists. What do exist are evidence-based skills and practices with a track record of successfully treating addiction. If you are ready, willing, open-minded, and honest with yourself, I believe Staying Sober will work for you.

When can I expect to feel better?

This is difficult to predict. Everyone's path is unique. There will ups and downs along the way. This is particularly true early on in sobriety. The healing process requires you to break old patterns of thinking, feeling, and behavior. Growing pains can be expected when you leave your old, addictive comfort zone. Remember, you set the pace of change. You are in control. Most people report they begin feeling better after a few weeks.

Why is this approach more effective than others?

Staying Sober is multidimensional. Treatment protocols integrate the most effective, evidence-based practices from the clinical/research community with the latest breakthroughs in addiction science, aspects of the 12-step model, and other spiritual/wisdom traditions.

Staying Sober's developmental approach makes treatment easier to implement. There are three major stages of recovery: Early, Mid, and Long-Term Recovery. Each stage focuses on distinct goals, tasks, skills, and activities.

- Early Recovery—I will teach you how to shift from addiction to recovery-based thinking, feeling, behaviors, and activities. You will learn coping tools to deal with the stressors that activate the addictive cycle.

- Mid Recovery—You will build on these skills by learning how to integrate these skills into a balanced, stable weekly routine.

- Long-Term Recovery—You will create an ongoing recovery maintenance plan to stay drug-free, one day at a time. I will also teach you the skills you need for ongoing personal growth and development.

CHAPTER 2

Guiding Principles of Staying Sober

Staying Sober is built on a new paradigm in addiction treatment called recovery management. Here are the guiding principles of this new treatment model that have been adopted by Staying Sober:

Addiction is a chronic, progressive medical condition that is cyclic in nature. This is described by the medical/mental health community as the "disease" model of addiction. In my view, this term is so loaded with negative cultural connotations that it is not helpful. I prefer a more judgment-neutral description that refers to addiction as a *chronic medical condition.*

Addiction can be successfully managed with proper treatment and ongoing aftercare. There is no cure for addiction at this time. However, like other chronic medical conditions—such as hypertension (high blood pressure,) asthma, diabetes, or arthritis—addiction can be successfully managed.

Staying Sober uses a developmental treatment model. Sobriety skills are introduced one at a time, so that each subsequent skill builds, reinforces, and strengthens the previous one. This creates a foundation for recovery that is solid and stable.

Staying Sober emphasizes personal empowerment. You are at the center of treatment. You assume responsibility for your recovery. You get to define what success means, choose your goals, and decide the pace at which you want to accomplish them.

Staying Sober is solution-focused, strength-based, and judgment-neutral. Staying Sober builds on your strengths. Treatment is built around your individual abilities. There are many roads to the mountaintop of sobriety. I invite you to use the path that resonates best with you.

Sobriety is a process, not a place. There is no finish line in recovery. Recovering addicts are engaged in the ongoing process of sobriety on a daily basis. The work does not end, but neither do the rewards!

Recovery is about managing, measuring, and tracking your progress. Staying Sober contains a built-in monitoring system (the Spectrum of Sobriety checklist) that enables you to measure and monitor the quality of your sobriety.

The Staying Sober Approach

Staying Sober begins with a simple idea. Whether it has been an hour, a day, a week, or more—the fact is right now, in this moment, you ARE sober. From this point forward, the work is about teaching you how to manage your recovery on a daily basis.

Addiction a complex, multifaceted condition that affects the way you think, feel, and behave. Staying Sober is similarly multidimensional, teaching you, step-by-step, how to change the way you think, feel, and behave. The focus of treatment begins with an understanding that the process is ongoing.

This represents a significant shift from previous treatment models that focus intensely, narrowly, and negatively on how to abstain from using and prevent relapse. This old approach uses a single episode, "one size fits all" type of programming over a short period of time. What we have learned, however, is that intensive, short-term treatment (thirty to forty-five days) produces short-term sobriety.

Staying Sober takes a different view. The focus is on developing an ongoing system of self-care that produces long-term sobriety. This developmental approach is designed so that each skill serves as a foundation on which the next one is built. Staying Sober is divided into three stages: Early Recovery, Mid Recovery, and Long-Term Recovery.

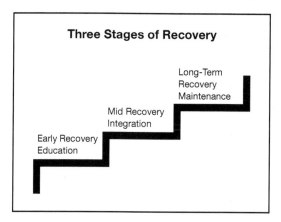

Three Stages of Recovery

Early Recovery: This is an educational stage. You will learn:
- Addiction is now understood to be a medical condition that is chronic, progressive and cyclic in nature (the medical model).
- The significance of the medical model on treatment.

- How the cycle of addiction operates and how to break it,
- How to shift from addictive-based to recovery-based thinking, feeling, and behaviors using 24 staying sober coping skills.

Mid Recovery: This is an organizing, integrating stage. You will learn how to:

- Organize new sobriety skills into a unified, balanced routine.
- Measure the *quality* of sobriety with the SOS checklist.
- Create a sober schedule.

Long-Term Recovery: This is a transformational stage. You will learn about the depth experience, how to address legacy issues, and the importance of practicing acts of service. You will learn how to:

- Shift from addictive to recovery-based lifestyle.
- Address unresolved issues, including childhood abuse/neglect or trauma.
- Understand the value of giving back, being of service to others, and making a positive contribution to community.
- Develop strategies for ongoing maintenance, living the dream of long-term sobriety, health, and wellness.

CHAPTER 3

The Medical Model
of Addiction

Recovery begins by recognizing that addiction is a chronic, progressive medical condition that is cyclic in nature. It is also important to understand that addiction presents like many other chronic medical conditions—including asthma, high blood pressure, or diabetes—and can be successfully managed with proper treatment and follow-up care.

Accepting addiction as a chronic, progressive brain condition is the bedrock on which Staying Sober builds its treatment model. If you do not accept that you have a chronic condition that requires ongoing symptom management, you are likely to drift back into denial and convince yourself that you can use alcohol or drugs the same way others do. The most dangerous four words a person in recovery can utter are, "I can handle this."

The truth is, addicts have great difficulty letting go of the deep, heartfelt desire to drink or use like "normal" people. I have yet to meet anyone in recovery who has not experienced this longing in one form or another. Researchers speculate this might be due to changes in brain structures that never entirely heal.

This might also explain why individuals with years—sometimes decades—of sobriety can suddenly find themselves overwhelmed by the desire to use. An insidious siren's song seems to call out "this time will be different."

"After all," the seductive voice of addiction whispers, "you have been sober for so long. You can handle it just this once. No one will ever know." Bill Wilson, the cofounder of AA, described this as the secret longing of all alcoholics: to be able to "drink like a gentleman."

Addiction Is *Not* a Choice

Acceptance of the medical model is also important to refute the misguided perception that addiction is a choice. Those who subscribe to this erroneous idea do so because they focus on the symptoms (such as the addict's self-destructive behavior) rather than the root, medical causes.

People who advise addicts to "just say no" believe that addicts will somehow learn to make better choices after suffering negative consequences. The reality could not be more different. One of the criteria of addiction is the continued use of addictive substances *despite* negative consequences!

The "choice" argument also carries judgment and blame. If using drugs or alcohol is a choice, then anyone who continues to use—regardless of the destructive consequences—must be somehow mentally ill, weak-willed, or morally flawed. This attitude is both inaccurate and damaging to addicts and those who love them.

Research from NIDA makes this point clear.

"For much of the past century, scientists studying drug abuse labored in the shadows of powerful myths and misconceptions about the nature of addiction. When scientists began to study addictive behavior in the 1930s, people addicted to drugs were thought to be morally flawed and lacking in willpower. Those views shaped society's responses to drug abuse, treating it as a moral failing rather than a health problem, which led to an emphasis on punishment rather than prevention and treatment. Today, thanks to science, our views and our responses to addiction and other substance use disorders have changed dramatically."

(From the National Institute on Drug Abuse website)

Accepting addiction as a chronic disease has profound implications for treatment. When we look at addiction from a medical perspective, we notice that it presents in ways similar to other chronic medical conditions. For example, relapse rates for many chronic illnesses, including addiction, are quite similar (see chart next page). We also know the symptoms of these chronic diseases can be successfully managed with proper treatment and ongoing care, maintenance, and monitoring.

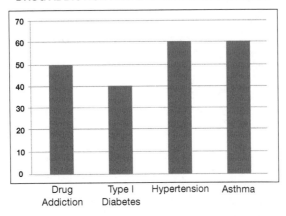

COMPARISON OF RELAPSE RATES BETWEEN DRUG ADDICTION AND OTHER CHRONIC ILLNESS

Relapse rates for drug-addicted patients are compared with those suffering from diabetes, hypertension, and asthma. Relapse is common and similar across these illnesses (as is adherence to medication). Thus, drug addiction should be treated like any other chronic illness, with relapse serving as a trigger for renewed intervention.

Source: JAW 284:1689-1695, 2000.

CHAPTER 4

The Cycle of Addiction and How to Break It

We now know that addiction is actually a medical condition that is chronic, progressive, and cyclic in nature. (For those interested in the neurochemistry of addiction, including its cyclic nature and the impact on the brain, please refer to PART SEVEN, "Clinician's Guide to Addiction Treatment.")

Stage 1: Stressors

Stress was originally a metallurgic term used to describe the tensile strength of steel and its ability to withstand constant pressure without buckling. It has since come to refer to the ongoing pressures of daily life and how they impact our physical, emotional, and psychological health.

Good Stress. Some stress is beneficial. The stress of meeting deadlines helps us become more productive and accountable. The

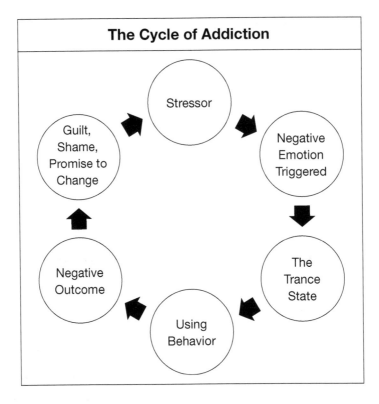

stress of competition often brings out the best in our performances. Good stress can actually inspire a person to achieve a goal or to become more confident or stronger physically.

Bad Stress. On the other hand, persistent levels of high stress can be devastating to our physical, emotional, and physiological well-being. Stress-related maladies range from tension headaches to ulcers and colitis, as well as major organ damage, depression, psychosis, and suicide.

The Law of Diminishing Returns

The law of diminishing returns describes how the effectiveness of stress to improve performance decreases the closer we come to peak performance. This principle also shows how ongoing stress can be counterproductive and decrease performance.

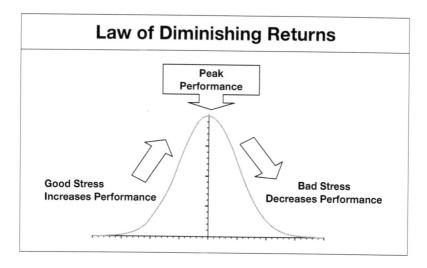

Stage 2: Negative Emotions Triggered

Stress activates negative emotions. Imagine you encounter a traffic jam on your way to work that will make you late for an important meeting. The stress created by this situation activates negative emotions, like frustration, fear, and anger. Left unchecked, these feelings can create a negative feedback loop. The more anxious you feel, the greater the negative emotional response. The greater the emotional response, the more anxious you feel.

As this process of rumination picks up speed and intensity, your deeply held, negative self-beliefs can also become activated. *Why am I always late? I never give myself enough time. I should have known I was going to hit traffic. I am such a moron!* We also experience physical symptoms of stress. Our heartbeat quickens. We feel flush or perspire. Our breath becomes rapid and shallow. We experience knots or butterflies in the stomach.

Stage 3: The Trance State

In the case of addiction, these physical and emotional symptoms are collectively referred to as post-acute withdrawal symptoms (PAWS). We will be discussing PAWS in great detail in PART FIVE, "Challenges in Recovery."

Factoid   **Euphoric Recall**

Refers to the formation and recollection of selected memories that highlight early, pleasurable drug or alcohol use experiences and edit out all of the pain, sickness, destruction, disappointment, or trapped feelings of addiction. This type of emotional editing leads to the delusion that using again will not lead to negative consequences but rather a much-desired relief of stress.

We try to avoid stress-activated, negative emotions by medicating them with drugs. This begins with a mental shift. We enter an altered state of consciousness I call the *trance state*.

It is like a fog rolls into our minds that interferes with our ability to think clearly. Often this shows up in a delusional state of nostalgia called *euphoric recall*. (See factoid box.)

Stage 4: Addictive Drug-Using Behavior

Once the trance state takes hold, it is extremely difficult to resist the craving to use. Adrenalin pours into the bloodstream. The body and mind are primed for the using experience. It is only a matter of time until the individual gains access/opportunity and drug use begins.

Stage 5: Negative Consequences

As soon as drugs enter the body, the pleasure/reward centers of the brain start to flood with dopamine and other neurochemicals. Communication between the executive brain functions—like risk assessment, impulse control, and decision making—become seriously compromised. The prefrontal cortex effectively goes offline.

The pleasure centers in the midbrain assume control. Decisions are determined by the amount of pleasure they produce or pain they avoid. As a result, behavior becomes increasingly unpredictable. Life starts to unravel. The speed and intensity of the unraveling might vary, but not its direction. Addictive behavior that continues over a significant time period results in negative consequences that become increasingly serious. They include:

Damage to physical health. The CDC reports that an average of 120 people die every day in the United States from acute drug overdose or conditions directly attributable to addiction. Other damage to physical health includes chronic and/or fatal diseases, such as heart attack, stroke, emphysema, cirrhosis, hepatic encephalopathy, hepatitis C, autoimmune diseases, and damage to the heart, lungs, liver, kidneys, and brain. Other types of physical damage also can occur due to erratic, high-risk actions and behavior while intoxicated (including car accidents, blacking/nodding out, tripping, stumbling, falling, fights, etc.).

Damage to relationships. This includes irresponsible, dishonest, selfish, manipulative, impulsive, aggressive, or violent behavior toward parents, partners, siblings, children, friends, and others. Broken relationships, separations, and divorces result.

Damage to finances/career/school. This might be caused by the inability to work to full potential, poor performance, getting fired, absenteeism, poor or failing grades, dropping out of school. Irresponsible, impulsive, or reckless financial decisions are often made when intoxicated. The money drain of maintaining a drug habit is often crippling.

Damage to rights, privileges, freedoms, and legal status. Negative consequences include DUI convictions and fines, infractions/violations of the law, civil lawsuits, arrests, time/money spent in court, restraining orders, probation, parole, time in jails or prisons, guardianship, and conservatorship.

Damage to mental health. This includes anxiety, depression, disorientation, cognitive deficits, memory loss, amnesia, blackouts,

---

Negative Consequences Inventory
(Check all that apply)

❑ Damage to career	❑ Damage to education/training
❑ Loss of job	❑ Damage to closest friendships
❑ Loss of professional license	❑ Physical injury (bruises, broken bones, hospitalizations)
❑ Suspension/loss of driver's license	❑ Chronic physical injury (cirrhosis, Hepatitis C, HIV)
❑ Arrest	❑ Damage to relationships
❑ DUI	❑ Damage/loss marriage
❑ Drug-related criminal activity	❑ Damage/loss home & finances
❑ Damage/Loss personal property	❑ Damage to emotional well-being (depression, anxiety, psychosis)
❑ Damage/Loss other people's property	❑ Chronic mental injury (neurological damage, "wet brain")
❑ Loss of freedom (prison, mental institution)	

---

brain damage, dementia, psychotic breaks, psychosis, schizophrenia, alcohol-induced delirium, sleep disorders, hallucinogen-induced disorders, and suicide. Time/money are spent on outpatient, inpatient, and long-term treatment and institutionalization.

Spiritual damage. One of the most insidious aspects of addiction is the shame and remorse generated by each successive addictive cycle. Every failed attempt to stop reinforces feelings of failure, hopelessness, and despair. A failure to be accountable to others, to keep promises, to be honest, and to live in integrity continues to erode the individual's self-esteem, self-worth, and self-love.

Stage 6: Guilt, Shame, Promise to Change

The addictive cycle seldom ends at a time and place of our own choosing. Generally, it takes a sufficiently negative consequence to interrupt the downward spiral. This can be when we run out of money or drugs, or we collapse from exhaustion. In many instances, the addictive cycle lands us in strange locations, not knowing how we got there: a hospital, ER, or jail.

Waking up after a drug binge tends to produce a moment of clarity. The veil of denial is ripped away and we are forced to confront the wreckage caused by our addictive behavior. This experience is emotionally overwhelming. *The Big Book of Alcoholics Anonymous* describes this as a "pitiful and incomprehensible demoralization."

I have certainly been there. At the end of a "run," I experienced huge waves of guilt, incredulity, confusion, humiliation, and shame crashing down on me. Alternating feelings of disbelief, self-loathing, disorientation, and despair circulated around and around in my brain.

It felt unbearable. *How could I have done this to myself again? What is wrong with me? Will I ever learn?*

> Non-addicts believe in God
> because they are afraid of hell;
>
> Addicts believe in God
> because they have been there.

It was hell on earth. I remember promising God—and anyone else who would listen—that I had learned my lesson and was ready to change. With every fiber of my being, I swore I was going to stay sober. I meant it with all my heart and soul! At times, I was able to string together days or even weeks of abstinence. But in the end, the stress-induced feelings of fear, anxiety, and my inability to cope overwhelmed my steadfast commitment and I felt pulled back into the gravitational orbit of the addictive cycle.

Breaking the Cycle of Addiction

In the section that follows, you will learn how to break the cycle of addiction using recovery-based skills, tools, tips, and techniques. I will teach you how to strategically deploy Early Recovery skills to interrupt the addictive cycle before the powerful trance state sets in and saps your resolve to stay sober.

Brain scans show how communication between the prefrontal cortex—the seat of executive functioning and impulse control—and the pleasure centers in the midbrain are compromised by stress.

You will learn how to listen to your body to recognize the signs of stress early enough to take a *contrary action*—to use a sobriety skill to avoid slipping into the trance state and eventually returning to drug or alcohol use. This is the key to breaking the cycle.

Once you take a contrary action and avoid using, a new cycle of sobriety emerges. Instead of using and having your life spin out of control, you make a recovery-centric choice, create a positive outcome, and experience an increase in self-esteem. Each time this is done, you reinforce a new Staying Sober cycle of behavior!

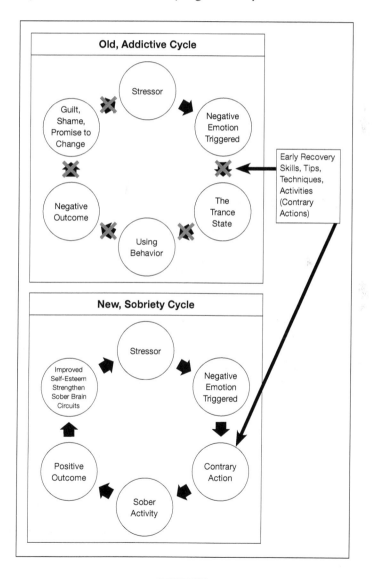

PART TWO

Early Recovery

*Learning the 24 Skills Needed to Shift from
Addictive to Recovery-Based Thinking,
Feeling, Behavior, and Activities*

Chapter 5: Cognitive-Based Sobriety Skills

Chapter 6: Mindfulness-Based Sobriety Skills

Chapter 7: Sobriety-Centric Behaviors

Chapter 8: Sobriety-Centric Activities

Cognitive-Based Sobriety Skills

Early recovery begins by teaching you how to shift the way you think and feel by replacing the addictive mind-set with recovery-based coping techniques. The skills we use to do this are generally referred to as cognitive, and focus on the way we think.

Cognitive skills help us restructure our perception (the way we see things and interpret what they mean) and shape the way we feel. Our emotional response to events then shapes our response or behavior. This is generally referred to as cognitive behavioral therapy (CBT).

Here are the cognitive skills we use to shift our thinking:

1. Training your mind to change your brain, using the CBT mood log to identify distortions and restructure thoughts.

2. Using the power of affirmations.

3. Cultivating an attitude of gratitude.

4. Reading daily meditation.

5. Journaling.

I will also introduce you to a powerful daily practice that promotes clarity of thought, healing in the brain, and improves mood and feelings of contentment: mindfulness.

Mindfulness is a modern adaptation of the ancient practice of breath meditation. Combining simple diaphragmatic breathing through the nose while focusing on staying in the moment promotes neurological healing, feelings of physical, emotional, spiritual well-being, as well as contentment and peace of mind.

Here are the mindfulness skills we use to promote emotional well-being:

6. Mindfulness meditation.
7. Visualization.
8. Mapping triggers with body scans.
9. The power of prayer.

Skill # 1 CBT

This skill set focuses on how to change our thinking. When we change the way we think, we change the way we feel and behave. This new understanding of the relationship between our thoughts and feelings was developed by Dr. Arnold Beck in the 1950s. He named this approach cognitive behavioral therapy (CBT).

CBT starts with the idea that what we think determines how we feel, which in turns determines how we choose to behave. In other words, the way we think about the events that take place in our lives is frequently the source of our distress.

CBT teaches us how to uncover the relationships among activating events, irrational beliefs, and self-destructive patterns of behavior. These irrational beliefs are called *cognitive distortions*. CBT also teaches us how to restructure our thoughts in ways that produce more accurate, rational beliefs and behaviors.

Learning the ABCs of CBT

The ABCs of CBT		
(A) Activating Event • Actual situation • Immediate thoughts • Initial interpretation	(B) Beliefs • Evaluation • Interpretation • Rational/Irrational	(C) Consequences • Emotions • Reaction/Response • Behavior

Activating event: The actual event and the client's immediate interpretations of the event.

Beliefs: The evaluation/interpretation of the event.

Consequences: The emotions and actions generated by interpretation.

Ten Major Cognitive Distortions

1. **All-or-nothing thinking.** You see things in black and white categories. If your performance falls short of perfection, you see yourself as a total failure.

2. **Overgeneralization.** You see a single negative event as a never-ending pattern of defeat.

3. **Mental filter.** You pick out a single negative detail and dwell on it exclusively so that your vision of all reality becomes darkened, like the drop of ink that discolors the entire beaker of water.

4. **Discounting the positive.** You reject positive experiences by insisting they "don't count" for some reason or other.

You maintain a negative belief that is contradicted by your everyday experiences.

5. **Jumping to conclusions.** You make a negative interpretation even though there are no definite facts that support your conclusion.

   A. **Mind reading.** You arbitrarily conclude that someone is reacting negatively to you and don't bother to check it out.

   B. **Fortune-telling.** You anticipate things will turn out badly and feel convinced that your prediction is an already-established fact.

6. **Magnification.** You exaggerate the importance of things (such as your goof-up or someone else's achievement), or you inappropriately shrink things until they appear tiny (your own desirable qualities or another's imperfections).

7. **Emotional reasoning.** You assume that your negative emotions necessarily reflect the way things really are: "I feel it, therefore it must be true."

8. **"Should statements."** You try to motivate yourself with "should" and "shouldn'ts," as if you had to be whipped and punished before you could be expected to do anything. "Musts" and "oughts" are also offenders. The emotional consequence is guilt. When you direct should statements toward others, you feel anger, frustration, and resentment.

9. **Labeling and mislabeling.** This is an extreme form of over-generalization. Instead of describing your error, you attach a negative label to yourself: "I'm a loser." When someone else's behavior rubs you the wrong way, you attach a negative label to him: "He's a moron!" Mislabeling involves describing an

event with language that is highly colored and emotionally loaded.

10. **Personalization and blame.** You see yourself as the cause of some negative external event for which, in fact, you were not primarily responsible.

(From *The Feeling Good Handbook* by David D. Burns, MD)

A CBT Exercise: Birthday Party Vignette

To illustrate how the same activating event can produce completely different emotional experiences and behavior based on distorted beliefs, read the following vignette and the two responses:

It is Betsy's birthday. Her parents decide to throw her a surprise party. They invite twenty of Betsy's friends as well as family members. Betsy's parents also cater the party and include some of her favorite desserts.

Betsy arrives home and is surprised. She spends the afternoon visiting with party attendees and eating lunch. Betsy receives gifts, cards, and phone calls from well-wishers. But one of Betsy's friends, Gwen, does not call.

Response # 1

I cannot believe my parents threw me a surprise party! How sweet! It caught me off guard at first, but I recovered when I saw all the smiling faces of my friends and family. My parents were so thoughtful to organize this party for me. They know birthdays can be hard for me. I feel lucky to have parents who put in the time, effort, and expense to celebrate important times in my life.

I cannot remember the last time I was surrounded by so many friends and family at the same time. It was hard to know whom to talk to first! What a good problem to have. I took a breath, relaxed, and got into the flow. Next thing I knew, I was comfortable and visited with everyone.

The food was amazing! My folks even remembered to get some of my favorite pastries. Yum! They were delicious. I ate too much. But, hey, if you can't splurge a little on your birthday, when can you? It was worth blowing my diet for the day. I will get back on my food plan tomorrow.

I noticed Gwen did not call. I wonder why. I know there is a flu going around. I hope she's not sick. Or maybe she is out of town on business. I know things have been hectic for Gwen after she was promoted. I have not talked to her in weeks. I think I will give her a call and see how she is doing.

List cognitive distortions you see in this response.

_____

_____

_____

_____

_____

Response # 2

I cannot believe my parents threw me a surprise party. It gave me a heart attack! They should know better than to surprise me like that. It made me so upset. I know everyone else in the world loves celebrating their birthday. I should, too. What is wrong with me? I am so screwed up.

Gwen did not even bother to call. I guess I am just not important anymore since she got her promotion. I should be moving ahead, like

Gwen. *Since everybody hates me at work, it will never happen. Everything is so political. Gwen and I used to be close, but I have not heard from her in weeks. It must be because she thinks I am just a lowly peon. It just goes to show how two-faced people are! If that is the way she wants to treat me, she can lose my phone number!*

Seeing friends was okay. But the only reason my family showed up is because they had to. I hate situations where I feel I have to visit with everyone. I managed to say hi to all the guests. I am sure some people felt slighted because I didn't spend more time with them.

The food was good, but as usual, my parents bought too much. They probably did it because they think all I eat is junk food. I cannot believe they bought all those fattening pastries. They know I can't resist them. I must have eaten 100 of them. I am such a pig! I should have more self-control, but I can't help myself. And it could not have come at a worse time. I started my new diet this week. What a joke. I must have gained ten pounds today! Who am I kidding, anyway, with this diet? I am never able to lose weight.

List cognitive distortions you see in this response.

_____

_____

_____

_____

_____

Using a CBT Mood Log

CBT mood logs use a simple, step-by-step process to help identify cognitive distortions and shift your mood by restructuring your thoughts. Look at the CBT mood log on the following page. All eight steps are numbered and described below. Follow along and learn how to use this helpful coping technique.

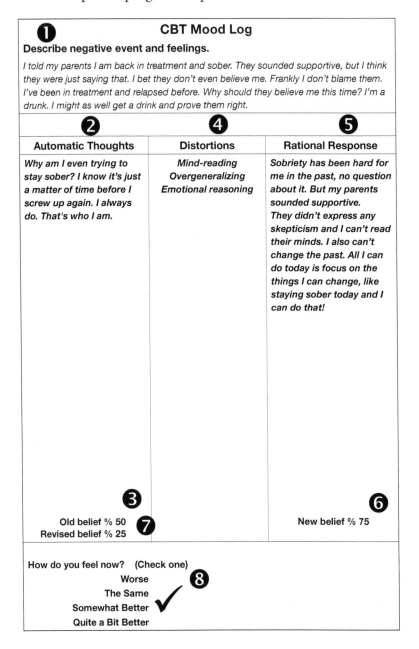

① CBT Mood Log

Describe negative event and feelings.

I told my parents I am back in treatment and sober. They sounded supportive, but I think they were just saying that. I bet they don't even believe me. Frankly I don't blame them. I've been in treatment and relapsed before. Why should they believe me this time? I'm a drunk. I might as well get a drink and prove them right.

② Automatic Thoughts	④ Distortions	⑤ Rational Response
Why am I even trying to stay sober? I know it's just a matter of time before I screw up again. I always do. That's who I am.	*Mind-reading* *Overgeneralizing* *Emotional reasoning*	*Sobriety has been hard for me in the past, no question about it. But my parents sounded supportive. They didn't express any skepticism and I can't read their minds. I also can't change the past. All I can do today is focus on the things I can change, like staying sober today and I can do that!*
③ Old belief % 50 ⑦ Revised belief % 25		⑥ New belief % 75

How do you feel now? (Check one)
Worse ⑧
The Same
Somewhat Better ✓
Quite a Bit Better

Step 1. Describe the negative event and feelings. He reports his feelings were hurt during a conversation with his parents. Though they sounded supportive of his recovery, he doubts their sincerity. He states this brought up feelings of inadequacy and self-doubt, which activated his desire to give up and use.

Step 2. Automatic thoughts. He writes the negative automatic thoughts and emotions triggered by his interpretation of the conversation.

Step 3. Old belief percentage. He rates how much he believes in that negative thought (50 percent).

Step 4. Distortions. He lists the cognitive distortions he engaged in. He realizes he was *mind reading*. He does not know for sure if his parents are skeptical. He also noticed he was *overgeneralizing* and *fortune telling*. Finally, he identified that he was engaging in *emotional reasoning*, confusing his feelings in the moment with reality.

Step 5. Rational response. He acknowledges the challenge of staying sober in a more rational way. He focuses on the things in his control, rather than out of his control, and uses a positive affirmation to keep things in perspective.

Step 6. New belief. He rates his rational response (75 percent).

Step 7. Revised belief. He compares his new belief to his old one and notes a 25 percent reduction in his negative thinking.

Step 8. How do you feel now? He reevaluates his mood and determines he is feeling "somewhat better" after completing the CBT mood log. (*More important, he did not go out and use!*)

CBT Mood Log by the Numbers

Now it is your turn! Use the step-by-step guide below to complete your CBT mood log on next page.

1. Describe a negative event or feeling. One or two sentences are fine. Use a recent negative feeling or situation.

2. Automatic thought. What did the voice inside your head immediately say?

3. Old belief percentage. On a scale of 1–100, rate how much you believe in that automatic thought.

4. Distortions. What cognitive distortions are active in this situation? Consult the list and identify the ones that apply to you. Often, more than one is activated. Distortions have a way of overlapping and clustering together.

5. Rational response. Now that you have identified the distortions, write a more thoughtful, rational response.

6. New belief percentage. On a scale of 1–100, rate your new belief.

7. Revised belief percentage. Deduct the new belief percentage from the old belief percentage.

8. How do you feel now? Reflect on how you are feeling right now. Compare your emotional state to the way you were feeling before completing the mood log. Check the box that describes your mood now.

❶ CBT Mood Log

Describe negative event and feelings.

❷ Automatic Thoughts	❹ Distortions	❺ Rational Response

❸

Old belief %
Revised belief % ❼

❻

New belief %

How do you feel now?   (Check one)
Worse ❽
The Same
Somewhat Better
Quite a Bit Better

Skill # 2 Affirmations

Affirmation is from the Latin term *ad ffirmare,* which means, "to make more firm." Affirmations are a simple yet powerful way to firm up, strengthen, and reinforce our recovery-based thinking, feeling, and behaviors. Essayist James Allen likened the daily firming up of positive thoughts to tending a garden.

"A man is literally *what he thinks,* his character being the complete sum of all his thoughts. . . . As the plant springs from, and could not be without, the seed, so every act of a man springs from the hidden seeds of thought, and could not have appeared without them.

Just as a gardener cultivates his plot, keeping it free from weeds, and growing the flowers and fruits which he requires, so may a man tend the garden of his mind, weeding out all the wrong, useless, and impure thoughts, and cultivating toward perfection the flowers and fruits of right, useful, and pure thoughts. By pursuing this process, a man sooner or later discovers that he is the master-gardener of his soul, the director of his life."

(From *As a Man Thinketh* by James Allen)

A more contemporary use of this metaphor is found in the highly popular book *The Four Agreements*:

"The human mind is like a fertile ground where seeds are continually being planted. The seeds are opinions, ideas, and concepts. You plant a seed, a thought, and it grows."

(From *The Four Agreements* by Don Miguel Ruiz)

The Power of Repetition

Affirmations draw much of their strength from repetition. We learn most things in life through repetition. Think about how we learned the multiplication tables. How much is 2 x 2? The answer, of course, is 4. The answer springs to mind without a moment's thought. The same is true for 3 x 3, 4 x 4, or 12 x12, (9, 16, 144.) How about when we ask how much is 13 x 19? This generally takes us a moment. We need to do the multiplication manually (or use our smart phones) to get the answer (247). Why? Because we only practiced our multiplication tables up to number 12.

Practice Makes Permanent

The power of repetition also applies to our beliefs about ourselves, particularly when we are young. Messages communicated to children (verbally and non-verbally) from birth to age seven have a profound effect on the development of important core beliefs. Are we lovable? Do we have value? Are we an accepted member of our family? Is the world a safe place? Can I care for myself? Can I trust others?

The more frequently messages about ourselves are repeated, the more ingrained they become. Over time, those ideas harden into the beliefs that inform our personality.

Addictive Core Beliefs

Patrick Carnes, PhD, asserts that, regardless of age, gender, color, or ethnicity, all addicts appear to share four negative core beliefs about themselves, others, and the world around them:

1. I am a bad* person.
2. If I show you who I am, you will leave/abandon me.

3. I can't trust anyone to meet my needs.

4. Using is my most important need.

* We all have our own version of this negative core belief, which could be expressed as *"I am unlovable, unworthy, unreliable, broken, evil, invisible, a loser, incapable, screwed up, dishonest, etc."*

Planting Positive Beliefs

Changing core beliefs begins by planting the seeds of sobriety in the form of positive affirmations. We cultivate these seeds with daily affirmations. This practice embeds new beliefs in our brain and helps them take root and grow.

Over time, these positive core beliefs break through the soil of consciousness and grow into the trunk and limbs of positive feelings and emotional resilience. And just as the fruit of the apple tree must be apples, daily practice of affirmations must manifest sobriety, health, and wellness!

Creating Positive Affirmations

Six Tips to Optimize Your Affirmations

1. **Make them personal.** Write your affirmations to address your specific needs. The most effective affirmations are the ones that come from the heart.

2. **Charge them emotionally.** The more your affirmations connect with your feelings, the more powerfully they will resonate inside you.

3. **Keep them in present tense.** Affirmations work best when grounded in the here and now.

The Tree of Sobriety, Health, and Wellness

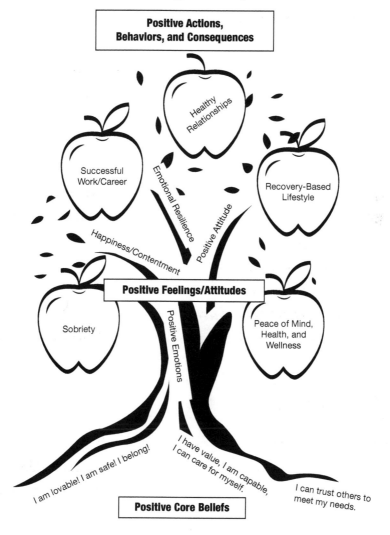

4. **Make them positive.** Formulate your affirmations as positive statements (that is, "I am sober" rather than "I am not using.")

5. **Be concise.** Short and sweet affirmations deliver the most power.

6. **Say them aloud three times a day.** Affirmations are meant to be said aloud with conviction!

Recovering Positive Traits

In our addiction, we tended to focus on our negative characteristics. The downward spiral of our using behaviors seemed to justify our negative view of ourselves.

Over time, many of us came to believe that we were nothing but our negative characteristics. We lost sight of our positive traits. In recovery, we have the opportunity to recover our positive personality traits.

Positive Personality Traits

Review these positive character traits (on next page) and circle the ones that apply to you.

Sobriety Affirmation Exercises

Positive Quality Affirmation

Write an affirmation based on one or more of your positive traits. Use ones you circled or come up with some of your own (for example, *I am a sensitive, caring person. I am insightful. I am kind to animals.*).

_____

_____

_____

Sobriety Affirmation

Write an affirmation that firms up and strengthens your recovery (for example, *I am sober today. My recovery grows stronger every day. I live in the sunshine of sobriety today.*).

_____

_____

_____

Accessible	Curious	Insightful	Respectful
Active	Decisive	Intelligent	Responsible
Adaptable	Dedicated	Intuitive	Romantic
Admirable	Disciplined	Kind	Secure
Adventurous	Dynamic	Logical	Selfless
Agreeable	Educated	Lovable	Sensitive
Alert	Empathetic	Loyal	Serious
Amiable	Energetic	Masculine	Sexy
Appreciative	Enthusiastic	Mature	Sharing
Articulate	Exciting	Methodical	Skillful
Athletic	Fair	Modest	Sober
Attractive	Faithful	Neat	Sociable
Balanced	Flexible	Open	Solid
Calm	Focused	Optimistic	Spontaneous
Capable	Forceful	Organized	Stable
Caring	Forgiving	Passionate	Strong
Charismatic	Friendly	Patient	Subtle
Charming	Fun-loving	Peaceful	Sweet
Cheerful	Generous	Perceptive	Sympathetic
Clean	Gentle	Persuasive	Thorough
Colorful	Genuine	Playful	Tidy
Compassionate	Good-natured	Practical	Tolerant
Conciliatory	Gracious	Precise	Trusting
Confident	Hardworking	Principled	Understanding
Conscientious	Healthy	Protective	Vivacious
Considerate	Helpful	Prudent	Warm
Contemplative	Honest	Punctual	Well-rounded
Cooperative	Humble	Rational	Wise
Courageous	Humorous	Realistic	Witty
Courteous	Idealistic	Reliable	Youthful
Creative	Imaginative	Resourceful	

Abundance Affirmation

Sobriety is the threshold we cross to arrive at a life of physical, emotional, and spiritual abundance! Write an affirmation about what abundance looks like to you. This affirmation is aspirational in nature (visualizing positive things to come.) Include material, physical, emotional, and spiritual abundance (for example, *Today I enjoy financial security, peace of mind, and healthy, loving relationships. I am healthy, happy, and free! My life is filled with love, laughter, and peace of mind.*).

_____

_____

_____

Skill # 3 Attitude of Gratitude

Gratitude comes from the Latin verb *gratis,* meaning "to freely give thanks." Psychology studies indicate that making a daily gratitude list might significantly improve our attitude, performance, and emotional resilience. It promotes feelings of wellness and contentment as well as a sense of abundance and emotional resilience. Grateful people tend to be happier, less depressed, less stressed, and more satisfied with their relationships.

Grateful people experience a greater sense of control over their environments, personal growth, purpose in life, and self-acceptance. Cultivating gratitude seems to generate more positive ways of coping with difficulties and increases the likelihood that they will seek support from others.

We Take So Much for Granted

It is easy for Americans (and many others in developed countries) to lose sight of just how good we have it. We enjoy a higher standard of living—as measured by life expectancy, health, wealth, and overall quality of life—than 95 percent of the world's population.

Here are just some of the things we take for granted:

- Safe permanent housing
- Protection from elements
- Clean water to drink
- Healthy food to eat
- Abundance of clothes, goods, and services
- Safety from physical harm
- Safety from political persecution
- Physical health—our senses, limbs, and muscles work properly.
- World-class medical care
- World-class technology
- Largest capital markets, job opportunities
- Freedom of assembly
- Freedom to practice religion

If I Have It So Good, Why Do I Feel So Bad?

In our addiction, we often found ourselves living in states of isolation, deprivation, and resentment. The rapacious nature of addiction has slowly eroded our ability to feel, cultivate relationships, and enjoy the abundance that surrounds us. This emotional vacuum was inevitably filled with feelings of fear, loneliness, and negativity. The spiritual practice of writing and reflecting on a daily gratitude list is a simple antidote to this kind of "stinkin' thinkin'."

Gratitude List Exercise

Purchase a journal in which to write your daily gratitude list. Begin each day by writing down a minimum of ten people, places, and/or things for which you are grateful. Be as specific as possible. List your friends and family members individually.

Review this list at night before bed and add additional items that occur to you. This is a daily practice. To keep it fresh, add new items to your list along with others you want to repeat. Push yourself to include little everyday people, places, and situations. You will be amazed at how much there is to be grateful for in recovery!

1.

2.

3.

4.

5.

6.

7.

8.

9.

10.

Skill # 4 Reading Daily Meditation

Reading an inspirational meditation in the morning sets a positive, recovery-oriented tone for the rest of the day. Practicing this one- to two-minute recovery skill is enormously helpful. I find if I read a daily mediation in the morning, my day is significantly less stressful.

For me, it has to do with the recognition that I can still experience small amounts of old, addictive emotions in the morning. They take the form of vague, hard-to-define feelings of dread and fear that show up about an hour after I get up in the morning. When I read a daily meditation within one hour of getting up, those old, addictive feelings do not appear that day.

Reading a daily meditation is like a daily immunization. It protects me from the emotional vestiges of my disease. I have no hard science to explain how this works. I only know it does work for me and millions of others in recovery. You can get daily meditation books at most bookstores, large 12-step meetings, or online. I suggest you give it a try!

Read the daily meditation below and see what comes up for you.

If you cannot get rid of the family skeleton, you might as well make it dance. —George Bernard Shaw

Many addicts come from families that are filled with secrets, lies, and shame that stretch back for generations. There are no open, honest exchanges among family members. Instead, there is a system of unspoken messages and shame. When we grow up in families where no one talks openly, we start to feel isolated and alone.

In our solitude, we sense something's wrong with us and come to believe we are the problem. With no one to challenge these distortions, our feelings harden into negative core beliefs about ourselves.

In recovery, we learn to break out of this isolation and shame by speaking openly and honestly about our families. If there are skeletons, we rattle them a little to shake things up. We even learn to laugh at the crazy world of shame and isolation that kept us disconnected from life. In talking and laughing we begin to break free.

Today I choose to break free from isolation and shame by speaking openly, honestly, and with a sense of humor.

Skill # 5 Journaling

The act of writing down your thoughts on a daily basis is a simple cognitive tool that promotes sobriety, health, and wellness. Writing about your thoughts will help you:

- **Clarify your thoughts and feelings.** Do you ever seem all jumbled up inside, unsure of what you want or feel? Taking a few minutes to jot down your thoughts and emotions (no editing!) will quickly get you in touch with your internal world.

- **Know yourself better.** By writing routinely, you will get to know what makes you feel happy and confident. You will also become clear about situations and people who are toxic for you—important information for your emotional well-being.

- **Reduce stress.** Writing about anger, sadness, and other painful emotions helps to release the intensity of these feelings. By doing so, you will feel calmer and better able to stay in the present.

- **Solve problems more effectively.** Typically, we problem solve from a left-brained, analytical perspective. But sometimes the answer can only be found by engaging right-brained creativity and intuition. Writing unlocks these other capabilities and affords the opportunity to discover unexpected solutions to seemingly unsolvable problems.

- **Resolve disagreements with others.** Writing about misunderstandings rather than stewing over them will help you to understand another's point of view. And you just might come up with a sensible resolution to the conflict.

Journaling's Psychological and Physical Benefits

Journaling is an activity that accesses the analytical, rational (left) side of your brain. Research indicates that when you engage the left brain in this way, your right brain is activated in ways that promote free, creative, intuitive, emotionally charged thoughts. As a result, journaling is a simple way for you to access all of your faculties to promote clarity of thought and improved mood.

Tips on How to Begin Journaling

Purchase a journal. The benefits of journaling are optimized by writing in longhand. I suggest you resist the temptation of journaling on the computer. Instead, go out and purchase a notebook or diary to use specifically for journaling. They are easy to find at any bookstore. While shopping for a journal, keep an eye out for one that somehow calls out to you. You are looking for a special place to collect your thoughts, feelings, and intuitions. Let that process begin by listening to your intuition when selecting your journal.

Journal freely. This is your special place where anything goes! Do not worry about spelling, punctuation, or sentence structure. Focus on allowing whatever is present in your thoughts, feelings, or intuition to tumble onto the page however it wants to.

Journal daily. It is less important what you write in your journal, and more important that you perform the simple act of writing something. Consistency over time is the key. One easy way to accomplish this is to open your journal, preferably at the same time every day, and record the date. If there is nothing specific on your mind at the moment, write about what it is like to feel stuck with nothing to say. If you stick with it for five minutes, something will always come out.

Journal privately, without judgment. Privacy is essential. Your journal is for your eyes only. Keep it in a safe place. Write freely. There are no censors, critics, or authority figures who will judge you. I find that early in the morning, before my internal critic wakes up, is a great time to spill my thoughts onto the page without fear of judgment or criticism.

Journal intimately. Think of your journal as an intimate friend who accepts you exactly as you are and wants nothing more than to hear what is going on inside you. There are no rules to journaling. Allow your mind and heart to guide your hand with as little interference as possible.

CHAPTER 6

Mindfulness-Based Sobriety Skills

The term "mindfulness" is a bit of a misnomer. When we hear the word, we often associate it with the cognitive process of being extra thoughtful or considerate.

The use of mindfulness here is quite different. At its most basic level, being mindful is about being present while engaging in diaphragmatic breathing. It is a state of mind in which we become aware of our thoughts, feelings, and sensations on a moment-to-moment basis. The goal of mindfulness is simply to notice the inner workings of our mind in a relaxed setting.

Skill # 6 Mindfulness Meditation

Mindfulness refers to the Buddhist practice of *vipassana*, which means insight or breath meditation. The Buddha developed this technique. He seems to have intuited the CBT idea that our interpretation of events distorts our thoughts and causes us suffering. Buddha developed mindfulness to intentionally slow the spontaneous thoughts, feelings, and sensations that come in and out of consciousness. He did this to experience the actual moment-to-moment phenomenon of being alive.

Mindfulness-based sobriety skills complement cognitive-based skills by providing us with the ability to experience all aspects of our thinking, feeling, and behavior without judgment or blame. This promotes self-soothing and self-acceptance.

In addition, mindfulness helps us notice our inner thought processes, which enables us to appropriately respond to situations rather than to mindlessly react. Finally, evidence-based research into mindfulness has determined that this practice activates the body's innate ability to heal itself in many important ways. See the list below.

Benefits of Mindfulness

- Improves concentration and cognitive acuity.
- Improves emotional resilience.
- Improves mood.
- Reduces cravings.
- Improves emotional well-being and contentment.
- Reduces depression and anxiety.
- Reduces impulsive, irrational behavior.
- Reduces symptoms of anxiety.
- Reduces symptoms of eating disorders.
- Reduces couples' conflicts.
- Reduces symptoms of anxiety disorders.
- Reduces symptoms of obsessive-compulsive disorder.
- Reduces/relieves symptoms of stress.

- Promotes healthy outcomes for those with heart disease.
- Promotes contentment and well-being.
- Lowers blood pressure.
- Reduces chronic pain.
- Improves sleep.
- Alleviates gastrointestinal difficulties.
- Promotes feelings of compassion, tolerance, and gratitude.
- Resets the autonomic nervous system to a relaxed state.

A Bit about the Breath

We take an average of 17,280 breaths a day without giving it a second thought. We refer to this as *tidal* breathing, the kind that fills the top third of our lungs.

Factoid **Diaphragmatic Breathing**

A form of breathing through the nose that utilizes the diaphragm, a long horizontal muscle that separates the lungs from the intestinal cavity. When the diaphragm is expanded, air is drawn down into the bottom of the lungs and is characterized by an expansion of the belly. Research confirms that the bottom 65 percent of the lungs have a preponderance of nerve receptors for dopamine, serotonin, GABA, and other naturally occurring chemicals in the body associated with pleasure, well-being, and contentment.

Mindfulness meditation includes diaphragmatic breathing. This type of breathing is slower, deeper, and more intentional than regular breathing. The object of this kind of breathing is to completely fill our lungs with air. Most of us are not accustomed to this type of breathing and have no idea just how large our lung capacity is.

Lung Capacity

If we took the entire surface area of our lungs and spread it out on the ground, it would be about 2,800 square feet. That is the same size as a tennis court!

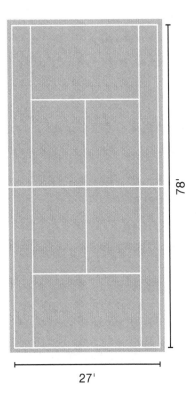

Nasal Breathing Is Healing

Our bodies are designed for nasal breathing. There are many medical and psychological benefits to breathing this way. Here is a partial list of those benefits.

- Kills bacteria, promotes health.
- Increases circulation.
- Improves lung volume.

- Retains body heat and moisture.
- Functions as an air conditioner to regulate body temperature.
- Increases mental capacity and enhances verbal ability.
- Provides more efficient way to extract oxygen from the air.
- Improves sleep.
- Improves pulmonary function.
- Improves cardiorespiratory fitness, posture, and respiratory muscle length.

Practicing Mindfulness

Learning how to become aware of your thoughts and feeling *in the moment*, without having to judge or do anything about it, is one key to long-term sobriety.

Why is this so important? Our thoughts, feelings, and sensations pop in and out of consciousness at an incredibly fast rate. We average 60,000 thoughts, feelings, or sensations per day. That breaks down to 3,750 per hour, 62.5 per minute, or 1.04 for every waking second of the day.

With mindfulness, no matter how intense or compelling our thoughts, feelings, or cravings might seem, *we know they will pass if we learn how to tolerate them without judgment or assigning them meaning.*

Instead of getting hooked by and reacting to negative emotions, we can simply *notice* them and allow them to drift out of our consciousness, like clouds passing across a clear blue sky.

This is very helpful for people in recovery. We learn to observe and tolerate our feelings without trying to avoid, control, or change them. We come to understand that we no longer have to self-medicate. We can now tolerate negative thoughts, feelings, or sensations we once found overwhelming.

Mindfulness teaches us how to tolerate feelings without having to "do" anything about them. We understand that feelings are not "facts" but rather momentary phenomena that we can observe without assigning meaning or judgment.

Mindfulness Exercise

Seven-Minute Guided Meditation: The Heart of the Ocean
(Listen to a free MP3 recording of this meditation
at: www.stayingsoberhandbook.com.)

Take a moment to check in with yourself. How are you feeling right now? Are you feeling a little tense, angry, or anxious? Contented, relaxed, and calm? Just so-so? Circle the number on the Mindfulness Meter below that is closest to your mood right now.

Mindfulness Meter
Circle the number to indicate how you are feeling.

Calm/Relaxed				Neutral			Anxious/Upset		
1	2	3	4	5	6	7	8	9	10

Let yourself get settled. If you can, it's good to sit with your back straight, feet planted on the floor, and legs uncrossed. If you need to lie flat on the floor, that's okay too.

With your eyes open, try letting your attention go to the middle of the room . . . and now just notice your attention as you let it go to the far wall . . . and now follow your attention as it comes back to the middle of the room . . . and then bring your focus up close, as if you are holding a book at reading distance. Notice how your attention can go many different places.

Now let your attention drift inward. Allow your eyes to close as you get a sense of the inside of your body as well as your body in space and where you are sitting in the room. And now, let yourself become aware of the sounds around you. Let the sense of sound fill your awareness.

Let your awareness find the breath wherever you feel it most prominently—whether at the level of your nostrils, the air going in and out, the level of your chest as it goes up and down, or the level of your abdomen going inward and outward. Perhaps you'll even notice your whole body breathing. Wherever it comes naturally, just let your awareness ride the wave of your in-breath, and then your out-breath.

When you notice, as often happens, that your mind might have wandered and become lost in a thought, a memory, a feeling, or a worry . . . simply make note of it and gently, lovingly return your awareness toward the breath—wherever you feel it—and follow the wave of the in-breath and the out-breath. Think of the breath as an anchor to which you can always return.

As you follow the breath, listen to this ancient story that has been passed down from generation to generation for thousands of years.

The mind is like the ocean. And deep in the ocean, far beneath the surface, it is calm and clear. Imagine you are sitting on the sandy ocean floor where all is calm and serene. You feel happy, at ease, and safe from harm. From this depth in the heart of the ocean, imagine yourself looking up. Notice the activity of the waves on the surface. No matter what the surface conditions are, whether it is flat or choppy or even a full gale storm, deep in the heart of the ocean it is always tranquil and serene.

Think of these waves as the brainwaves on the surface of your mind. Imagine that your thoughts, feelings, and sensations, whether calm or stormy, remain on the surface—and that deep below, in the heart of the ocean, you are calm, safe, and at ease.

If random thoughts, memories, or sensations catch your attention, simply notice them and return to the breath. It might be helpful to name these thoughts as a way of letting them go before returning your attention to the breath and following it as it rides inward and outward from this deep, tranquil place. Let's ride the waves of breath inward and outward from this deep, tranquil place a few more moments.

This serene, spiritual place is available to us as often as we like. Take a few more breaths here and imagine the heart of the ocean as a place that resides somewhere in your body, perhaps in your heart or your lungs, or tucked away in a secret place that only you know. With your next inhale, deepen your breath slightly. Slowly wiggle your fingers or toes and slowly begin to return to the room. When you are ready, slowly open your eyes.

Return to the Mindfulness Meter and circle the number that is closest to your mood right now.

Skill # 7 Visualization

The conscious mind—the part that is reading the words on this page right now—represents about 10 percent of total consciousness. The remaining 90 percent operates below the level of conscious thought. We refer to this vast region of the brain as the unconscious. One of the unique aspects of the unconscious is that it does not distinguish among actual experience, memory, or the imagination. All three are experienced as real and taking place in the present in the realm of the unconscious.

A famous experiment conducted the early 1970s illustrates this point. A college basketball team was divided into three groups. The first group was instructed to practice shooting free throws for an additional thirty minutes a day. The second group was instructed to *visualize* shooting free throws for thirty minutes a day. The third group was told to do neither.

After two weeks, the team assembled and shot free throws. The players who had practiced shooting free throws had improved 30 percent. The players who had visualized shooting free throws had improved 35 percent! The players who did neither stayed about the same.

Why Visualization Works

When we visualize ourselves living drug-free, happy, and free, the experience gets imprinted on our memory as though it is actually happening. Just like affirmations, the more we repeat this process, the stronger and more real it becomes. Think of visualization as a video clip you can play over and over in your mind, knowing that each time it is repeated, its transformational power is at work in your psyche.

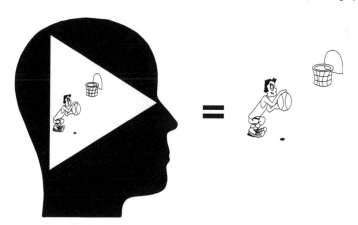

Visualization Exercise

Find a comfortable, quiet spot where you will not be disturbed. Close your eyes. In your mind's eye, picture yourself waking up in the morning rested, refreshed, and excited about the day. See yourself reading and writing your morning gratitude list. Imagine yourself peeking over your shoulder and watching yourself write each thing for which you are grateful.

Watch yourself rise to your feet as you prepare to recite your daily affirmations. Feel the muscles in your legs flex as you stand. Experience the ground underneath your feet. Is it hard wood? Carpet? Listen to the conviction in your voice as you hear yourself saying your affirmations aloud.

Imagine surveying your space as you prepare for the day. Your bed is made; everything is organized, neat, and clean. You are dressed appropriately for the day. See yourself step into your day upbeat, relaxed, and confident. See yourself moving effortlessly through the events of the day. You are sober, happy, and energetic. You gracefully overcome obstacles, resolve problems, and accomplish all of your goals for the day.

Next, imagine sitting down to dinner with a partner, friend, or family member. You eat, chat, and laugh as you share the events of the day with this person.

Now turn your mind's eye to a visual of the evening. You are unwinding and ready for bed. You see yourself reflecting on the day. You feel contentment and a sense of well-being. You listen to your thoughts. "I stayed sober today! I did not lie, steal, cheat, or manipulate anyone. I can do this tomorrow, the day after, and the day after that. I can stay sober and enjoy an amazing life!" See yourself turning off the bedroom light, closing your eyes, and drifting off into peaceful, restful sleep.

As you end your visualization, take a moment to thank yourself for taking the time to give yourself this visualized gift.

Skill # 8 Mapping Triggers with Body Scan

In the movie *The Godfather*, family patriarch Don Corleone advises his sons "to keep your friends close, *but keep your enemies closer.*" The same is true for the people, places, and things that "trigger" or activate the cycle of addiction.

By "keeping our enemy closer," we mean keeping a keen eye out for the stressful thoughts, feelings, and sensations that trigger us. We use the spiritual tool of mindful awareness to monitor our moment-to-moment experience and alert us when we experience the early signs of feeling triggered.

Recovering Our Ability to Feel

In our addiction, we used drugs and alcohol to avoid our feelings. As our using progressed, we medicated our feelings when we felt bad, when we felt good, or when we felt bored. Numbing or medicating our feelings with our drug of choice (DOC) became a way of life.

In sobriety, we begin to recover our capacity to feel. We are in the process of learning non-using coping skills to feel our feelings. We recover our emotions by learning how to listen to our bodies.

Our bodies are constantly sending us signals about our ever-shifting physical and emotional states. Our bodies signal when we are hungry, tired, angry, scared, or anxious. It is important for us to learn how to recognize these signals, particularly the ones that appear when we feel triggered to use.

Examining Your Triggers

Each of us experiences triggers differently. The same thoughts, feelings, and sensations can be triggering to some and not others. What is important is that we learn to identify *our* triggers.

On the list below, circle the thoughts, feelings, and sensations you experience when you feel triggered to use. Please feel free to add to this list. Be as specific and thorough as possible.

Triggering Thoughts, Feelings, and Sensations

- Quick, shallow breathing
- Weak, rapid heartbeat
- Mouth watering
- Dry mouth/throat
- Constriction in the chest area
- Butterflies in stomach
- Twinges, tension in the belly
- "Bubble guts"—the need to go to bathroom
- Tingling sensations
- Sharp or painful sensations
- Perspiration, feeling flush, warm
- Feeling "amped up," the rush of adrenalin
- Numbness, dissociated, "out of body" experience
- Inability to concentrate, loss of interest in work/school
- Highly focused on where, how, and when to use
- Obsessive thought patterns
- Manipulative behavior
- Sexually stimulated
- Feeling lightheaded
- Behaving in a secretive, deceptive, dishonest manner
- Easily agitated, irritated, upset, nervous, or tense
- Retreating into fantasy

- Loss of interest in relationships, responsibilities
- Selective "euphoric recall" around using experiences
- Anticipation about the prospect of using
- Antsy, fidgety, difficulty standing or sitting still
- Catatonic
- Feeling a sensation of falling, disappearing
- Emptiness, numbness
- (*add your own here*)
-
-

Mapping Your Triggers Exercise

The best way to learn what it feels like to be triggered is to identify where the triggering sensations show up in our bodies. Use multicolored pencils, pens, or crayons to illustrate where they show up in your body and what they feel like.

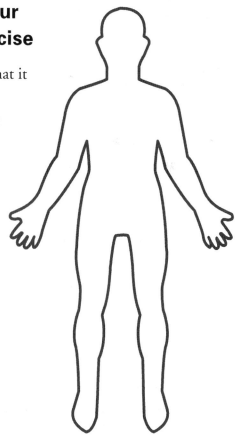

Skill # 9 The Power of Prayer

Prayer and meditation are ancient, time-honored spiritual tools. There are thousands of varieties of these spiritual practices. Prayers can be said silently or aloud; in groups or alone; they can be spoken or sung; recited in conjunction with rituals or by themselves. They can be done sitting still, walking, or engaging in any type of movement. What they all share in common, however, is a conscious effort to make a spiritual connection with a power greater than ourselves.

In *How God Changes Your Brain*, Andrew Newberg and Mark Robert Waldman make a remarkably simple observation. The limits of science and human understanding make it impossible to prove or disprove the existence of God. What can be accurately measured, however, is "the effect that religious beliefs and experiences have on the human brain."

In other words, regardless of whether or not God *actually* exists, engaging in spiritual practices such as prayer and meditation create measurable changes in the neuronal circuitry of the brain.

Three Major Findings

1. Spiritual practices, even when stripped of religious beliefs, **enhance the neural functioning** of the brain in ways that improve physical and emotional health.

2. Intense, long-term contemplation of God and other spiritual values appears to **permanently change** the structure of those parts of the brain that control our moods, give rise to our conscious notion of self, and shape our sensory perceptions of the world.

3. Contemplative practices **strengthen a specific neurological circuit** that generates peacefulness, social awareness, and compassion for others. (**Bold** emphasis added.)

(From *How God Changes Your Brain* by Andrew Newberg and Mark Robert Waldman)

Other health benefits of spiritual practices include improved cognition, impulse control, and the ability to cope with stress. On average, people who engage in regular spiritual practices enjoy a higher quality of life as measured by longevity and more satisfying careers, work and social relationships, and marriages and partnerships.

Changing the Prayer Paradigm

Many of us were introduced to prayer in childhood. In most cases, we were taught "penitent" prayer. In this form of prayer, we ask or petition God to show us mercy, restore our health, or provide some type of material or emotional support. This relationship is hierarchical in nature, like the one between parent and child.

Factoid	**Higher Power (HP)**
For the purposes of our discussion, I am using HP to refer to God, Higher Power, Higher Purpose, your fellowship, or whatever conception you have of a power greater than yourself.	

Re-Visioning Your Approach to Prayer

Staying Sober invites you to explore another way to think about the nature and function of prayer. For the next few minutes, see if you can clear your mind of your old assumptions about God and religion. Consider what it would be like to have a new perspective on this issue. Instead of feeling like a hopeless, helpless child petitioning or pleading with God to solve your problems, imagine creating a more adult partnership arrangement.

"When I was a child, I spoke like a child, I thought like a child, I reasoned like a child. When I became a man, I gave up childish ways."

(From 1 Corinthians 13:11)

Partnership with Your Higher Power (HP)

Imagine developing a new deal or partnership with HP. This partnership is *interdependent*, meaning both partners need to work together. Instead of a hierarchy, the partnership is more about the division of labor. On a daily basis, HP removes the problems that interfere with your sobriety so that you can show up in your life as the best, most authentic version of yourself.

That's it! I do my part; HP does its part. Together, we create the best, sober version of me possible. This enables us to "stay in our lane" and focus on the things we can control and change.

Simple, yet not easy. Where does our stuff end and HP begin? This is where the practice of prayer and meditation are so valuable. These spiritual tools help us decide what to work on and what to let go of. Here are some examples of prayers that address this issue.

The Third Step Prayer

"God, I offer myself to Thee—To build with me and to do with me as Thou wilt. Relieve me of the bondage of self, that I may better do Thy will. Take away my difficulties, that victory over them may bear witness to those I would help of

Thy Power, Thy Love, and Thy Way of life. May I do Thy will always! Amen"

(From *The Big Book of AA*)

The Seventh Step Prayer

"My Creator, I am now willing that You should have all of me, good and bad. I pray that You now remove from me every single defect of character which stands in the way of my usefulness to You and my fellows. Grant me strength, as I go out from here, to do Your bidding. Amen"

(From *The Big Book of AA*)

Serenity Prayer

God, grant me the serenity to accept the things I cannot change,
The courage to change the things I can,
And the wisdom to know the difference.

Here's the rest of the prayer.

Living one day at a time.
Enjoying one moment at a time.
Accepting hardship as a pathway to peace.
Taking, as Jesus did,
This sinful world as it is,
Not as I would have it,
Trusting that You will make all things right,
If I surrender to Your will,
So that I may be reasonably happy in this life,
And supremely happy with You forever in the next.
Amen.

(Attributed to Reinhold Niebuhr)

Factoid   **Who Wrote the Serenity Prayer?**

The serenity prayer was excerpted from a sermon written by American theologian Karl Paul Reinhold Niebuhr (1892–1971). Ruth Hock Crecelius, the secretary of AA's Central Office (and first paid employee) read the sermon in the newspaper and brought it to Bill Wilson's attention. Wilson liked it so much, he printed the first verse on business cards and handed them out to people who wanted to understand AA's approach to spirituality.

Perhaps the most beautiful example of developing an interdependent relationship with the HP of your understanding comes to us from St. Francis of Assisi, a fascinating historical as well as religious figure. In 1204, this bright, handsome, and healthy son of the aristocracy marched off to war. He returned a few years later, a shell of his former self. (Today we might view this as a case of posttraumatic stress disorder, PTSD).

His response to the trauma of war was to reject his noble birth and life of privilege. He decided instead to devote his life to helping others. In his prayer, below, we see the same dynamic as in the previous prayers: God, please channel your energy through me so I can be the best version of myself possible. While this prayer grows out of the Christian faith tradition, I believe its message of interdependency, compassion, and service is universal and transcends its sectarian roots.

Prayer of St. Francis of Assisi

Lord, make me a channel of thy peace—

that where there is hatred, I may bring love—

that where there is wrong, I may bring the spirit of
forgiveness—

that where there is discord, I may bring harmony—

that where there is error, I may bring truth—

that where there is doubt, I may bring faith—

that where there is despair, I may bring hope—

that where there are shadows, I may bring light—

that where there is sadness, I may bring joy.

Lord, grant that I may seek rather to comfort than to be
comforted—

To understand, than to be understood—

To love, than to be loved.

For it is by self-forgetting that one finds.

It is by forgiving that one is forgiven.

It is by dying that one awakens to Eternal Life.

Amen.

CHAPTER 7

Sobriety-Centric Behaviors

These behaviors are where the rubber hits the road in Early Recovery. They are specific things to do and activities to participate in.

Skill # 10 Boundary Setting

Most friends and family members are willing to do what they can to support our new, drug-free lifestyle. There might be others who partially support our recovery. But there also will be those who will not support our sobriety.

Those who choose not to support our sobriety tend to be people who are still actively using. This might be because our recovery holds up a mirror to their untreated addictive behavior. This can be very uncomfortable or threatening to them. We might notice these people drifting away over time or becoming reluctant to make changes in their own lives to support our recovery.

We are not in the business of telling anyone else how to live. What we need to do, however, is set clear boundaries to protect our fragile, new recovery. Everyone's situation is unique. Relationships are seldom black and white. Here is a simple way to organize the people, places, and things in your lives into three general categories.

The Three Circles of Sobriety

Inner Circle—Avoid

People, places, and things that do not promote your recovery. Old dealers, using friends, romantic connections we used with, clubs, bars, and other venues you associate with using.

Middle Circle—Engage with Caution and a Safety Plan

People, places, and things that partially promote your recovery. This might include friends and family members who drink, favorite restaurants, or business and social functions at which people drink and use. We need to exercise caution and common sense when navigating these situations. Come up with a safety plan to help you attend while still protecting your sobriety; for example, attending with a sober friend, setting a time limit on your visit, or "book-ending"—calling your sponsor before and after the event.

Outer Circle—Spend as Much Time as Possible

People, places, and things that actively promote your recovery. This is where we want to spend most of our time. The Outer Circle of people, places, and things is infinite and should continue to grow in recovery.

A Sober Circles Exercise

Reflect on your current family, living, working, and school relationships. Put each individual in the appropriate circle. Do the same for other areas in your life, including places you like to go and things you like to do.

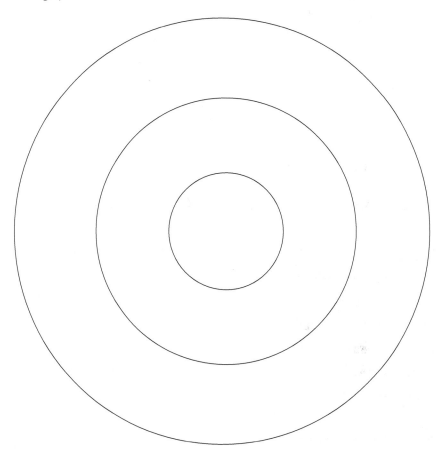

Skill # 11 Sober Home/Work/School

Look around your space. Are there drug- or using-related posters, paintings, or other items in your living space? This is a good time to replace items you associate with your old, negative, using patterns.

Changing the look and feel of your space shifts the energy and reinforces the positive changes you are making. You might want to replace pieces of furniture, particularly if they are dirty or have cigarette burns, stains, or other using-related damage. If replacing the item is not financially realistic, consider reupholstering or covering furniture with something colorful or recovery-centric.

Can you rearrange the furniture to give your place a new look and feel? You might be surprised how changing the position of where you sit changes your perspective.

Remove Drug/Alcohol Paraphernalia

This is also a good time to get rid of the beer bottle or shot glass collection. The same is true for your hookah, bong, pill crusher, using-related mirrors, spoons, lighters, etc. Replace using-associated items, such as drug/alcohol-related paintings, pictures, or posters on the wall.

How about a new coat of paint? Replacing old curtains, drapes, or rugs? Cleaning the windows, emptying out cluttered drawers? Your personal space is a reflection of your psychological state. Begin the process of getting your outsides to match your insides!

Sober Roommates

For those living with others, maintaining a clean and sober living space can be complicated. Before we got sober, many of us chose to live with people who use. Now that we are in recovery, we recognize the need to live in a place that supports our recovery. How do we address this situation with roommates/housemates and partners?

Ideally, you live with outer circle people who actively support your sobriety. They will understand that you need to live in a clean and sober environment and will honor that boundary by not using in the space you share. It also means they will not keep drugs or alcohol in the home.

In many cases, our living situation includes a mixture of outer circle and middle circle elements. For example, a roommate might support your recovery but still take prescription medication. Your roommate might have using friends or partners who visit. Your housemates might even occasionally throw parties at which alcohol is served.

Open and honest communication is always best when discussing your recovery with roommates. You might explain to them that your sobriety has to come first to you. That means living in a place that is drug-free. Make it clear you do not want to tell them how to live. Rather, you want to find out how willing they are to support your recovery.

If they are willing to meet your needs, great! If not, you might have to make alternative arrangements. Either way, it is important that we stay out of the judgment/blame game. Remember, we are the ones who are changing. Get as much support and feedback as possible from sober people whose opinions you trust before having this discussion.

Figuring out how to navigate your living situation early in sobriety can be tricky. Be sure to consult people who fully support your recovery before you make any changes. The guiding principles in this area are: safety first and keep it simple.

For those returning to work or school, participating in these activities sober might be a new or novel experience. As addicts, many of us found ways to use while at work or school. Decide which activities you will need to avoid in the workplace. These might include: drinks with coworkers at lunch, or after work; entertaining clients; and attending business functions, conferences, conventions, music venues, or other environments at which drugs and alcohol are present.

There is no "one size fits all" solution to maintaining sober work/school environments. What is required is a thoughtful, case-by-case review of triggering situations and the development of strategies about how best to handle them. People who are already in recovery can be a great source of advice about managing your work and school life while maintaining sobriety.

Skill # 12 Personal Appearance/Hygiene

Important, non-using coping skills that are often overlooked in early sobriety include the way we maintain our personal space, appearance, and hygiene. It is often shocking to see pictures of ourselves taken when we were active in addiction. The pain and misery of our inner state can be seen in our facial expression, posture, physical condition, and clothing as well as the way we maintained our personal space.

You Are What You Wear

Our appearance and dress are reflections of who we are. This takes many forms. Appropriate dress for your work environment will be different from what you wear to the beach—unless you are a lifeguard. The point here is, there is a relationship between what we wear in public with the venue in which we are wearing it.

In our addiction, many of us dressed in ways appropriate to the drug culture in which we were living. Some of these looks were thuggish or threatening; others were flamboyant or sexually provocative. Whatever drug-culture mask you wore, I invite you to reflect on your dress and appearance. Do they accurately reflect who you are today? Are there changes you can make that better reflect your new lifestyle?

This is a sensitive area. I am not the fashion police. I am suggesting you think about how managing your appearance can be a skill to promote positive change in your recovery.

"First I make up my bed, then I make up my mind!"

This quote from Robert Frost has always stuck in my mind. I like the no-nonsense, New England practicality used to explain the importance of cleaning your personal space first thing, to clear your mind for the day.

Look at the checklist of sobriety-centric personal maintenance and hygiene practices. I believe maintaining a clean living environment and practicing healthy personal hygiene are every bit as important to sobriety as daily affirmations or writing a daily gratitude list.

Appearance and Hygiene Checklist

Daily

- ✓ Make bed.
- ✓ Pick up all clothing/items off the floor.
- ✓ Put all dirty clothes in laundry bag.
- ✓ Shower/bathe (morning or night before).
- ✓ Use deodorant.
- ✓ Brush teeth (morning and night) and floss.
- ✓ Shave/ maintain facial hair.
- ✓ Apply after-shave or make-up (if appropriate).
- ✓ Trim and maintain clean fingernails and toenails
- ✓ Comb/groom your hair.
- ✓ Dress in clean clothes that are in good repair. Clean, fix, or discard clothing that is stained, torn, or otherwise inappropriate.

✓ Clean plates, utensils, and glasses. Do not leave dirty dishes in the sink!

✓ Inspect yourself in the mirror before leaving the house.

Weekly

✓ Dust, vacuum, and clean your personal space.

✓ Wash your clothes and neatly put them away.

As Needed

✓ Maintain your car in good working order (oil checks, service maintenance).

✓ Wash/clean your car inside and out.

✓ Haircut.

✓ Manicure.

Skill # 13 Self-Soothing Behaviors

Self-soothing behaviors are healthy, short-term actions, techniques, and strategies we use to calm and center ourselves in the moment. Establishing new, healthy ways to soothe ourselves when we feel hungry, angry, lonely, tired, bored, scared, or overwhelmed is essential to maintain recovery. For long-term sobriety, self-*care* refers to longer-term, systemic behaviors, like diet, exercise, or your morning spiritual practice.

Developing healthy self-care and self-soothing behaviors is very important in recovery. Now that we have stopped using drugs or alcohol to medicate our feelings, we need to find new, healthy ways to discharge negative stress. Unless we perform ongoing self-care and self-soothing, we can easily get out of balance and set ourselves up to relapse.

For better or worse, our using behavior served an important function for many years: keeping negative emotions and beliefs at bay. To suddenly remove this deep-seated coping mechanism and not replace it with something as effective would be like removing a broken cornerstone from a building and not replacing it with a new one. The building would become unstable and ultimately come crashing down.

Breaking old patterns of behavior can be challenging. When we begin to replace old, addictive responses with new, healthier ones, it can feel strange, boring, or downright uncomfortable—at first. This is where patience and persistence play an important role in keeping us on task while we make this adjustment.

Physical Exercise

What kind of physical activities can you use to care for and soothe yourself? Be specific. Instead of "exercise," figure out exactly what kind suits you. Lifting weights? Aerobics? Jogging? Tennis? Dance classes? Gardening? Yoga?

Exercise Tips

- Pick physical activities you like, not ones you think you should do.
- Make sure it's fun to do.
- Start slowly, and don't overdo it.
- Find physical activities you can do with others (because it keeps you motivated and accountable).
- Stick with it, even when you don't feel like it.

Other Types of Physical Self-Soothing

Grooming is a great form of personal self-care. How about treating yourself to a weekly manicure or pedicure? What about a therapeutic massage? Maybe you can take a hot bath as a way to unwind and soothe yourself after a full day.

Mental/Emotional Self-Soothing

When we are mentally or emotionally run down and need to recharge, some of us need quiet and solitude, while others need connection and interaction with others. Know what works best to keep you in balance.

Take a walk in nature. Read a book, do a crossword or jigsaw puzzle, or Sudoku. Keep a journal, listen to music, go to a museum, knit/crochet, watch your favorite TV show, have a cup of tea; you get the idea.

Self-Soothing Activities with Others

Call the person "you've been meaning to talk to," and make plans to meet up with sober friends before or after a meeting. Go bowling, play softball, or find other weekly activities at which your presence is expected. Create a weekly "date" night with your partner, or schedule a Sunday dinner with family and friends.

Spiritual Self-Care

Find activities to deepen and restore your spiritual relationships. This can be done by taking a walk at places of special significance, attending services at a house of worship, or being of services to others.

Exercise: A Self-Soothing Inventory

List self-care/self-soothing activities you can commit to for the next twenty-one days. Why three weeks? Because it takes about twenty-one days to transform an activity into a habit!

1.

2.

3.

4.

5.

6.

7.

8.

9.

10.

Skill # 14 Healthy Diet and Nutrition

There is a renewed interest in diet and nutrition across all areas of public health today. We appear to be eating more, gaining more weight, and becoming less well-nourished. The reasons standing behind these troubling trends go well beyond the confines of this book. But it is significant to note that addictive behavior and lifestyle exacerbates this problem in two ways.

- The substance itself affects the body.
- Using causes negative lifestyle changes, such as irregular eating and poor diet.

The National Institutes of Health (NIH) identifies additional problems. The researchers point out that addictions interfere with the body's natural ability to regulate metabolism (transforming food into energy), as well as affecting organ function and the immune system, The type and severity of damage due to poor diet and nutrition varies, depending on the class of drug, length and frequency of use, and other factors.

Opiates

Opiates (including codeine, oxycodone, heroin, and morphine) affect the gastrointestinal system. Constipation is a very common symptom of substance use. Symptoms that are common during withdrawal include:

- Diarrhea
- Nausea
- Vomiting

These symptoms might lead to a lack of enough nutrients and an imbalance of electrolytes (vital minerals, such as sodium, potassium, and chloride).

Eating balanced meals might make these symptoms less severe; however, eating can be difficult, due to nausea. A high-fiber diet with plenty of complex carbohydrates (such as whole grains, vegetables, peas, and beans) is recommended.

Alcohol

Alcoholism is a major cause of nutritional deficiency in the United States, according to the NIH. Common nutritional deficiencies include low levels of pyridoxine (vitamin B6), thiamine, and folic acid. These deficiencies can cause anemia and neurological problems. The lack of thiamine that results from prolonged, heavy drinking is the cause of the Wernicke-Korsakoff syndrome ("wet brain").

Alcohol use also damages two major organs involved in metabolism and nutrition: the liver and the pancreas. The liver removes toxins and other harmful substances from the body. The pancreas regulates blood sugar and the absorption of fat. Damage to these two organs can cause an imbalance of fluids, calories, protein, and electrolytes.

Other alcohol-related nutritional complications include:

- Diabetes
- High blood pressure
- Permanent liver damage (or cirrhosis)
- Seizures
- Severe malnutrition
- Shortened life expectancy

Marijuana

Acute Adverse Effects of Marijuana Use

- Impaired short-term memory, making it harder to learn and retain information.
- Impaired motor coordination, interfering with driving skills and increasing the risk of injuries.
- Impaired judgment, which can lead to high-risk sexual behaviors/STDs.
- In high doses—paranoia and even psychosis.

Long-Term Effects of Chronic and/or Heavy Marijuana Use

- Gateway to addiction. Marijuana is the first drug used for about 9 percent of all users; 17 percent of teens; and 25–50 percent of daily users.

- Altered brain development in adolescents/teens.
- Poorer educational outcomes, including dropping out of school.
- Cognitive impairments. Marijuana lowers the IQs of daily-user teens.
- Diminished life satisfaction and achievement (as determined by subjective and objective indicators).
- Chronic bronchitis symptoms.
- Risk of chronic psychosis (schizophrenia) in vulnerable individuals.

The most serious long-term effects are strongly associated with marijuana use that begins during adolescence.

Stimulants

The use of stimulants—such as crack, cocaine, and methamphetamine—reduces appetite and leads to weight loss and poor nutrition. Users of these drugs might not sleep for days at a time. They might become dehydrated and have electrolyte imbalances during periods of drug use. Returning to a normal diet can be hard if a person has lost a lot of weight. Memory problems, which might become permanent, are a complication of long-term stimulant use.

Damage to Teeth and Gums

Smoking methamphetamine or crack can seriously damage teeth and gums. The combination of exposure to heat, dehydration, and poor oral hygiene can result in gum disease, tooth decay, and tooth loss.

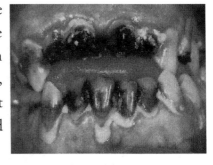

Diet and Nutrition Impact Mental Health

Balanced nutrition helps improve mood and health. Eating nutritious meals three times a day also promotes a recovery-centric schedule. Performing healthy behaviors consistently, over time, is an important way to reinforce a sober lifestyle. But someone who has just given up an important source of pleasure might not be ready to make other drastic lifestyle changes. It is more important that we avoid returning to substance use than that we stick with a strict diet.

Guidelines

- Stay hydrated.
- Stick to regular mealtimes.
- Include two health snacks per day.
- Eat foods that are low in fat.
- Eat more protein, complex carbohydrates, and dietary fiber.
- Vitamin and mineral supplements might be helpful during recovery (this might include B-complex, zinc, and vitamins A and C). Ask your healthcare provider.
- Get physical activity and enough rest.
- Reduce caffeine and stop smoking, if possible.
- Seek help from counselors or support groups on a regular basis.

(From the National Institutes of Health)

CHAPTER 8

Sobriety-Centric Activities

Skill # 15 Attend Support Group Meetings/AA

Changing activities begins with connecting with a sober community. There are many built-in benefits to participating in a sober community. In the case of AA, there are meetings everywhere. The fellowship has lots of sober activities in which to participate. You can come and go as you please. And it is free!

AA and Other 12-Step Fellowships

Alcoholics Anonymous is the oldest, largest, and most stable sober support fellowship in the United States. AA started in 1935. Since that time, more than 165 other support fellowships have been established using the same 12-step model of recovery. These include organizations like Narcotics Anonymous, Cocaine Anonymous, Nicotine

Anonymous, Gamblers Anonymous, Sex Addicts Anonymous, Debtors Anonymous, and Overeaters Anonymous, to name a few.

Spirituality ≠ Religion

AA and other 12-step fellowships are spiritually based programs. This is often misconstrued to mean that AA is a religion or religious-based organization. This is not the case. AA literature states this explicitly.

> "AA is not a religious organization nor is it affiliated with any religious body. It welcomes members of all religions, agnostics and atheists alike. You don't have to sign up or achieve anything to be a member. You're a member of a group if you choose to be. You can come and go as you please. No one is "in charge" of a group. We work through the offer of help and suggestion only. No one can tell you what you should or shouldn't do."

(From the pamphlet, *Is AA For You?*)

A Brief History of Spirituality in AA

It was Swiss psychiatrist Dr. Carl Gustav Jung who indirectly introduced the idea of a spiritual solution for alcoholism to the cofounder of AA, Bill Wilson. There is an account of this in *The Big Book of Alcoholics Anonymous* by Dr. Bob Smith and Bill Wilson. Dr. Jung had treated a patient named Rowland Hazard for alcoholism. After a period of sobriety, Rowland relapsed and returned to Jung for additional treatment.

Jung told the patient what he needed was a "vital spiritual experience." The psychiatrist went on to describe the nature of this phenomenon as a type of huge emotional displacement in which old ideas are cast out and new ones take their place. Never once in this account does Jung refer to this as a "religious" experience, nor does he ever use the word God.

Without putting too fine a point on this, the 12-step model recognizes that the disease of addiction is chronic and requires ongoing treatment in the form of support groups, fellowship, and activities with others in recovery.

Why I Prefer the 12-Step Model

I will confess a bias toward 12 step-based fellowships. To begin, the 12-step model of AA is everywhere. At last report, there are AA meetings being held in 120 countries around the world! Here in Los Angeles, for example, there are more than 5,000 AA meetings held weekly. This number does not even include the hundreds of other 12-step fellowships that conduct weekly meetings (for example, NA, CA, GA, SAA, OA, etc.).

The 12-step model promotes the idea of newcomers working with more experienced members who act as sponsors or guides to help newcomers learn the steps of the program. This relationship is offered at no cost and is completely voluntary.

People enter into sponsorship relationships freely and are free to leave at any time. The basic premise is that sponsorship is mutually beneficial. The newcomer learns how to use the tools of the 12-step approach to stay sober; the sponsor strengthens his or her own sobriety by being of service. It is a remarkably simple, win/win relationship.

The 12 Steps of Alcoholics Anonymous

1. We admitted we were powerless over alcohol—that our lives had become unmanageable.

2. Came to believe that a Power greater than ourselves could restore us to sanity.

3. Made a decision to turn our will and our lives over to the care of God *as we understood Him.*

4. Made a searching and fearless moral inventory of ourselves.

5. Admitted to God, to ourselves, and to another human being the exact nature of our wrongs.

6. Were entirely ready to have God remove all these defects of character.

7. Humbly asked Him to remove our shortcomings.

8. Made a list of all persons we had harmed, and became willing to make amends to them all.

9. Made direct amends to such people wherever possible, except when to do so would injure them or others.

10. Continued to take personal inventory, and when we were wrong, promptly admitted it.

11. Sought through prayer and meditation to improve our conscious contact with God *as we understood Him,* praying only for knowledge of His will for us and the power to carry that out.

12. Having had a spiritual awakening as the result of these steps, we tried to carry this message to alcoholics, and to practice these principles in all our affairs (*italics* in original text).

(From Chapter 5, *Alcoholics Anonymous*)

Attending AA Meetings

A good rule of thumb for those new to recovery is to attend three to five meetings a week. It is a good idea to mix things up and attend different types of meetings. For example, if you are going to start out with three meetings a week, include a speaker meeting, a *Big Book*/12-Step Study meeting, and a meeting where the members focus on open sharing and participation.

One thing I can promise you about 12-step meetings is this: you will like some better than others. My advice is to return to the ones you like and skip the ones you do not. I like to think of this as a form of meeting shopping. Drop into different meetings until you find three that you like and that fit into your schedule. To learn more about the different types of meetings and when they are held, log on to the local AA website in your area.

Picking a Sponsor

There is a tradition in AA called sponsorship. This is a relationship between a newcomer and someone who is sober and has been in the program a while. The role of a sponsor, strictly speaking, is to "take you through the steps" of AA. This means to teach you how to implement the tools of the program and to offer his or her "experience, strength, and hope."

Sponsor/sponsee relationships are unique. Everyone does it a bit differently. What all of these types of relationships share are:

1. Newcomers select the person they want to sponsor them. You retain complete control over whom you choose to act as your sponsor.
2. It is voluntary. Both people agree to work together.
3. The relationship is free.
4. The sponsor and sponsee have the right to end the relationship at any time for any reason.

Developing a relationship with a sponsor can be invaluable. In addition to being taken through the steps, sponsors act as sounding boards. They offer the wisdom of their experience, strength, and hope in recovery. Sponsors can also be great resources to find out about sober activities.

Skill # 16 Sober Support Network Individual Therapy

Once you stop self-medicating, it is not long before long-suppressed feelings, sensations, memories, and resentments, begin to surface. It is very important to have a mental health professional who specializes in addiction to help you work through these issues.

A well-trained therapist can also be extremely valuable by helping you repair and renegotiate broken or damaged relationships. Most therapists also work with couples and families or offer groups for people in recovery.

When shopping for a therapist, here are some important things you might want to ask:

- Are they trained in treating addiction?
- Why did they choose to work with addicts/alcoholics?
- Are they personally in recovery?
- Are they familiar with the 12-step model?
- How do they feel about treating someone who attends AA meetings?

Types of Therapy

When therapy issues involve others, consider using clinicians who specialize in couples and families or who run specialized groups. For those with budgetary constraints, attending group therapy is a viable alternative to individual therapy.

Psychiatrists and Medication

Some people suffer from underlying psychological conditions as well as addiction. In many cases, these conditions can be effectively treated with medication. The role of the psychiatrist is to assess whether medication is indicated to treat psychological distress. When appropriate, psychiatrists will prescribe a medication and monitor your condition on a regular basis. When selecting a psychiatrist, be sure they are addiction-savvy. Disclose that you are in recovery and cannot take any addictive or habit-forming medications.

Physicians and Other Medical Professionals

Many people recovering from addiction have not received medical care in quite some time. Locate a primary care physician and have a physical examination. Be sure you are examined by other medical specialists as well. Formulate a plan for any needed follow-up care; if necessary, research programs that can make such care available within your budgetary constraints.

Skill # 17 Sober FUN!

It is very important for us to have fun early in sobriety. Unless we experience some measure of fun, satisfaction, and release of tension, we will erroneously conclude that sobriety feels worse than using drugs, which can lead to relapse.

In our addiction, we drained our bodies of naturally produced pleasure chemicals, including dopamine, serotonin, and oxytocin. We relied instead on taking substances that multiplied the effect of these chemicals. It can take months before your body is able to produce and regulate the production and release of dopamine.

While this is going on, most of us experience anhedonia: a feeling of emotional flatness where nothing seems fun or interesting. We are bored, easily irritated, and temporarily unable to experience normal joy and happiness. Engaging in fun activities actually speeds up dopamine production in the body, reducing this temporary emotional lull.

Fun in Sobriety?

The idea of sober fun might sound like a contradiction in terms for some. After all, the entire reason for getting high was to experience pleasure, which came to be synonymous with having fun, right? We did as many things while high as possible. It can take some trial and error and experimentation with life on your new life's terms to find ways to have fun while sober.

A good place to look for fun activities is AA meetings. In meetings of any size, people tend to get together and share meals before and/or after meetings. Chances are good you will meet people with similar interests and background with whom to spend time.

Get Physical

One of the fastest ways to help your body resume dopamine production is physical exercise. It does not matter what type. What matters is engaging in physical activity that elevates your heart rate for thirty to forty-five minutes daily. Any activity during which you find yourself breathing a little harder and deeper is fine to start.

Rediscover Old Hobbies and Interests

Which activities gave you pleasure earlier in your life? Playing an instrument? Working in the garden? Writing? Reading? Dancing? Baking? Try rekindling your interest in an old hobby.

It often is helpful to think back to the last time you were happy. What were you doing? It is okay to go back as far as you need to find pleasurable activities. In the case of Carl Jung, he returned to childhood activities of playing with tin soldiers and building forts to rekindle his capacity for joy.

Try New Things

Still struggling to do something fun? Try something new. It is more important to try something than to sit back, get negative, and do nothing. On a whim, I went online and searched for "fun activities." Google came back with "about 573,000,000 results." Here are twenty I picked at random.

1. See a movie at the drive-in.
2. Walk on the boardwalk and listen to the boards creak under your feet.
3. Blow bubbles.
4. Play tag, hopscotch, or one of your favorite childhood games.
5. Ride a roller coaster.
6. Play miniature golf.
7. Win a prize at the fair.
8. Catch fireflies at night.
9. Build a sandcastle at the beach.
10. Eat a whole lobster with your hands.
11. Pick berries and peaches at a farm.
12. Buy a treat from the neighborhood store.
13. Roast marshmallows over a fire and make s'mores.
14. Make lemonade from scratch.
15. Sip a sweating glass of iced tea.
16. Eat a slice of watermelon.

17. Buy fresh produce at the farmers' market.
18. Nap in a hammock.
19. Have a picnic in the park.
20. Play an instrument.
21. Listen to music.
22. Knit a sweater.
23. Call a friend.
24. Clean out the closet, attic, garage.
25. Dance, sing, express yourself creatively.

The point here is, get active! The sooner you do, the sooner you will start feeling better!

Skill # 18 Active Listening

Communicating your feeling and needs in appropriate ways is an important skill to cultivate in recovery. Most of us are out of practice. In our addiction, we spent most of our time splitting off, numbing, or obliterating our feelings with using behaviors. As we grow in recovery, we learn how to become emotionally articulate about our own feelings and how to be good listeners when others share.

How We Communicate

We communicate in many ways. In fact, studies suggest that words convey the least amount of meaning when we communicate with others! The pyramid of communication illustrates this phenomenon.

Verbal—Meaning conveyed by the words used.

Para-Verbal—Meaning conveyed by the tone of voice, emphasis, words per minute, and phrasing.

Non-Verbal—Meaning conveyed by facial expression, eye contact, body language, other non-verbal cues.

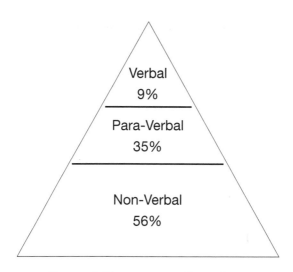

Good Communication

Good communication starts with good listening. Four active listening skills that promote good interpersonal communication are mirroring, non-verbal cues, validating phrases, and empathic open-ended questions.

Mirroring: Requires reflecting back what you hear as accurately as possible and then checking in to see if you got it right. (For example, "What I hear you saying is . . . Is that right?")

Non-verbal cues: Steady eye contact, engaged posture, open body language, nods, smiles, and appropriate facial gestures show you're paying attention.

Validating phrases: When appropriate, respond with phrases that indicate you are "tracking." (For example, "I hear you." "Really?" "Wow!" "I feel you." "I'm sorry to hear that.")

Empathic, open-ended questions: Imagining what another person is feeling based on what he or she is saying. (For example, "Wow, that must have made you feel great!" "I am so sorry, that must feel awful.")

Bad Communication

Many of us developed bad communication habits to keep people at bay, to avoid taking responsibility for our actions, or to keep secrets. Do any of these bad habits sound familiar to you?

Giving advice: Most times, people simply need to be heard and acknowledged. Don't offer advice unless asked. No one likes unsolicited advice or being lectured to. Avoid saying things like, "I'll tell you what your problem is . . ."

Making it all about you: Keep the focus on the other person. Don't hijack the conversation to talk about yourself or "one-up" their story. (For example, "Yes, I've been to Paris. I was there last year. I had so much fun." OR "You think *you* hit bottom? My bottom was lower than yours!")

Judging, shaming, or blaming: Making judgmental remarks. (For example, "Why did you do that?" or "That's one of the stupidest things I've ever heard.")

Active Listening Exercise

Most of us are not even aware we are engaging in behaviors like advice giving, making it about us, or shaming/blaming when we communicate. It takes a conscious effort to spot these behaviors in order to change them.

Do you find these behaviors come out more with certain people? Are you often giving advice to family members? Hijacking your conversations with some business or social contacts? Blaming or shaming certain friends? Where do we notice these tendencies come out—at the office, school, gym, or social venues?

Answer the following questions after thoughtful reflection.

People/relationships with whom I tend to engage in advice giving, making it about me, or shaming/blaming/judging. What can I do differently?

_____

_____

_____

Places/situations at which I notice myself engaging in these behaviors. How can I handle these situations differently?

_____

_____

_____

Skill # 19 Assertive Communications

Learning how to ask others for help or to get our needs met is extremely important. Now that we are sober and not medicating our feelings, we must learn how to express/process them in healthier, more appropriate ways. Appropriate modes of communication might not have been modeled for us at home. They might have fallen into three negative communication styles:

Aggressive Style

This communication style relies on bullying, threatening, and dominating others verbally. This can include yelling, screaming, name-calling, making threatening gestures or facial expressions, using profanity, foot stomping, fist pounding, or throwing/breaking things.

Aggressive communication seldom gets people to sympathize with you or makes them want to help you. In most cases, aggression breeds resentment and distrust.

Passive Style

Passive communicators tend to speak just above a whisper. They avoid eye contact and have slumped, withdrawn posture. They use self-blaming language like, "I know it is all my fault" or "I am such a loser." Passive communicators might demonstrate an inability to maintain eye contact.

Passive/Aggressive Style

This style relies on sarcasm, irony, or stony silence and emotional withdrawal to communicate feelings. Also referred to as "kidding on the square," the passive/aggressive speaker might cloak emotions like anger or sadness in humorous remarks. Passive/aggressive people try to get their needs met by manipulating us with feelings of guilt or obligation.

"If you don't want to include me in your plans, that's fine. Have a good time. Don't worry about me. I'll be fine sitting here all alone tonight with nothing to do and nowhere to go."

Developing an Assertive Communication Style

This is the most effective way for us to ask to get our needs met and express our feelings to others. This style is straightforward. We take responsibility for our feelings by "keeping statements in I." One easy way to describe assertive communication is to break it down into three parts: "When you _____, I feel _____. I need _____."

Here is an example of how it works.

Vignette

Imagine you have asked a friend to take you to a meeting and she agrees to take you. Other people contact you and offer you a ride. You turn them down because you have already made travel arrangements. Instead of being picked up at the agreed time, your phone rings. It is your friend saying she has changed her plans and will not be able to take you to the meeting after all.

You might reply:

"*When you* agreed to take me to the meeting, I turned down other ride offers so I could go with you."

"Because you changed your plans at the last minute and didn't let me know in time to make other arrangements, *I feel* like an afterthought. *I feel* slighted, hurt, and very upset that you do not take my feelings into consideration."

"*I need* to develop relationships with people who are impeccable with their word and considerate of my feelings. I have no other way of getting to the meeting tonight, and meetings are a very important part of my recovery plan. I need you to keep your word and take me to the meeting."

Assertive Communication Tips

- Avoid profanity, raising your voice, or shaming/blaming.

- State your needs in a straightforward way.

- Keep statements in the "I" as much as possible.

- Adapt the terms "When you, I feel, I need" into language with which you are comfortable.

An Assertive Communication Exercise

Write down a recent conversation in which you did not get your needs met or did not communicate effectively.

Describe the conversation.

_____

_____

_____

Circle communication modes/styles you notice.

Giving advice; making it all about you; shaming/blaming; using profanity; raising your voice; being aggressive/threatening; being passive/playing the victim; being sarcastic or ironic; being manipulative.

Restate your position in the assertive style.

When you—(State the events as plainly and unemotionally as possible.)

_____

_____

_____

I feel/I felt—(Be direct and keep it in the "I.")

_____

_____

_____

What I need—(Again, use direct unemotional language to describe the importance of getting this need met.)

_____

_____

_____

Skill # 20 Dealing with Resentments

Resentments are an insidious form of anger and bitterness that take up residency in our mind where they fester and grow. Unless we learn how to let go of resentment, it has a tendency to cycle around in our heads. We ruminate on the nature of the perceived wrong done to us. With each revolution, the resentment grows, triggering increasingly negative emotions and laying the foundational justification for us to use.

Factoid 💡 **Resentment**

From the Latin words *re* (to experience again with intensity) and *sentire* (to sense or feel). Resentment is a mixture of anger, fear, and feeling of injustice. AA considers resentments "The number one offender" and major cause of relapse.

Holding a resentment is like taking poison and expecting the other person to get sick!

Overcoming Resentments

Resentments are often connected with old, deep-seated cognitive distortions that tend to cluster together or constellate into negative beliefs, moods, or attitudes. They are often complex and require time and patience to tease apart and resolve.

Because handling resentments is so important for those in recovery, there is no shortage of pop-psychology advice about how to deal with them—but much of it is inaccurate or just plain wrong. Here are two common misconceptions about how to deal with resentments, which you must avoid:

The Spiritual By-Pass
(Praying Resentments Away)

You might hear the best way to deal with resentments is to turn it over to your HP. This can be an effective short-term strategy, but is no substitute for examining the underlying causes and conditions of the resentment. This includes identifying the way(s) you contributed to the problem.

Trying to Deny, Ignore,
or Push Resentments Away

Attempting to deny, discount, or avoid feeling resentments only makes them more problematic. Jung summed this up aptly: "That which we deny possesses us." When we deny or ignore a resentment, it gets to burrow into shadowy regions of the unconscious. At some point, this resentment inevitably resurfaces, stronger and more negative than before.

Dealing with Resentments

The first and most important thing to remember about resentments is: **Do not make a mess.**

Try not to react in ways that will make the situation worse. Use the mindfulness diaphragmatic breathing technique to regulate your emotions and do not overreact. Do what you need to do to remove yourself from the person, place or thing that triggered the resentment.

The PRINT Solution

PRINT is an acronym for a helpful process to work through stressful, destabilizing emotions. It stands for:

Purge (put it out there): Find an individual or group with whom you can vent your resentful feelings and let 'em rip! This is about getting ALL your feelings out on the table.

Reality check: Ask for and remain open to the feedback of others about their take on the situation.

Investigate: Explore the underlying causes and conditions that triggered the intense feelings of resentment.

Next step: Work out a plan to avoid, minimize, or cope with the resentment in the future to reduce its negative impact on you.

Take action: Implement your plan. Adjust and fine-tune as needed and report back to your support group on the results.

PRINT is covered in much greater detail in Chapter 19, "Overcoming PAWS with PRINTS."

Skill # 21 Making Amends

Saying you are sorry is not the same as making amends. As addicts and alcoholics, most of us have been apologizing for our behavior for years. After a while, our apologies begin to ring hollow. They are meaningless because, shortly after saying how sorry we are for our selfish, dishonest, and self-destructive behavior, we go out and do it again.

Making amends is fundamentally different from an apology in a number of ways. First, the intention of amends is not about saying you are sorry or asking for forgiveness.

The Difference between Amends and Apology

Making amends requires a few specific steps:

1. Take responsibility for the consequences of your actions. Address only your part. Do not indulge in assessing the

behavior of others. Focus exclusively on "cleaning up your side of the street."

2. Name the specific nature of the behavior for which you are making amends, acknowledge it was wrong, and then apologize. (For example, "Raising my voice and calling you stupid was wrong of me. I am very sorry I said that.")

3. Identify the exact behavior that caused the problem and state your commitment to changing the behavior. (For example, "I realize I am impatient and judgmental. I am committed to changing these behaviors.")

4. Ask if there is anything you can do right now to make things better.

Conspicuously absent from the amends process is asking for forgiveness. This is a key point. In order for them to be effective, *amends must be offered with no expectation of reward.* The purpose is for us to clean up our mess in order to stay sober, period.

If the person wants to give you feedback after you finish your amends, listen but do not become defensive or react in any way. Helpful, neutral responses include phrases like, "I can see how you feel that way," "Thank you for telling me that," and "I appreciate your honesty."

Tips on Making Amends

- Ask permission. Before making your amends, tell the individual you wish to speak to him or her and ask for a convenient day/time to talk privately.

- Stay calm. Amends are best made in a calm, nonjudgmental tone of voice.

- Be brief and prepared. It is a good idea to figure out exactly what you are going to say, and practice it before actually making the amends. This will help you avoid getting tongue-tied or losing your train of thought.

- Do not react. There is no way to tell how the other individual will react. He is entitled to his feelings and will respond accordingly. Regardless of what he says, DO NOT REACT, become defensive, or engage in debate.

Example of amends for a partner or friend:

Hi Alice, I need to make amends for my behavior last night. I am learning in my recovery program that I need to be accountable for my behavior and when I do something wrong, I need to clean it up right away. I picked a fight with you last night about the grocery bill and called you stupid and irresponsible. I was thoughtless, hurtful, and completely out of line. That was wrong of me and I apologize. I realize I have a fear of financial insecurity that interferes with my relationship with you. I am actively working to improve in this area. Again, I am so sorry. Can I do anything right now to help you feel better?

Example of financial amends:

Hi Joe. I want to make amends to you for my behavior last week. I am in a program of recovery from alcoholism, which tells me I need to take responsibility for my behavior in order to stay sober. When we were out at dinner last week, I called you an asshole and a cheapskate for not picking up the tab for dinner and I bullied you into paying. That was selfish, manipulative, and wrong. I am deeply sorry. I have learned I have a problem being selfish and inconsiderate of others and I am working on improving in these areas. Here is the money for my portion of dinner. Once again, I apologize. Is there anything else I can do to make things better between us?

An Amends Exercise

Describe a person to whom you owe amends. (*Tip—Start off with an amends that is small and manageable.*)

_____

_____

_____

State the exact nature of what you said/did wrong. Say "that was wrong" and apologize simply.

_____

_____

_____

Name the issue/s underlying the thing you said/did (for example, "I have a problem with patience and considering the needs of others") and state your commitment to working on changing the behavior.

_____

_____

_____

Ask if there is anything you can do right now to make things better. That is it! You are done. Your amends is complete.

If the other individual wants to respond in some way, let her. DO NOT become reactive, defensive, or try to explain/justify your behavior. The most important thing is to not undo the important work you just accomplished by creating another mess. When she is done, you can respond by saying, "Thank you for telling me that," "I understand how you feel," or "I appreciate the feedback."

Skill # 22 Bookending

Bookending is a way of beginning and ending the day with recovery practices. Specifically, we use the same sobriety skills we practiced in the morning to review our day before going to bed. This practice is a good way to frame, contain, and reinforce our sober intentions and keep them top-of-mind. Bookending, in one form or another, is a part of most spiritual/wisdom traditions, including AA. You can find a detailed description of AA's approach to bookending in *The Big Book of AA*.

As you get ready for bed, set aside a few minutes to review the events of the day. Ask yourself,

- Did I stay sober?
- Did I get triggered to use? If so, how did I handle it? Is there anything I might do differently?
- Did I practice self-care? Did I use my skills to stay emotionally centered? Was I on-task and accountable? Did I lie, cheat, steal, manipulate, or hurt anyone? If so, what do I need to do tomorrow to make amends?

Review the gratitude list you wrote that morning. Are there any items on the list that stand out as being particularly meaningful or significant? Any additional people, places, or things you experienced during the day for which you are grateful? Any other items you want to add to your list in the morning?

Finally, acknowledge and honor yourself for staying sober. Some days are more challenging than others. There are times when it feels like the desire to use is stalking us like our shadow. Other days, we don't even think about picking up once. At the end of the day, it really doesn't matter whether it was easy or hard. What matters is that we stayed sober today! Since all we have is today, we accomplished our goal.

Skill # 23 Taking Contrary Actions

Run Toward the Roar

In his book, *The World Behind The World*, Michael Meade shares a story from an African wisdom tradition about the importance of facing your fears. African tribal elders tell this story to young men coming of age. They advise young people to "run toward the roar" when they hear the lion's threat. It is often better to face the fear than run away.

Lions travel in prides (packs), led by an alpha male. After years of ferociously ripping and tearing, the alpha male lion loses his canines and front teeth. Though this makes his bite considerably less dangerous, the absence of these teeth enlarges the lion's oral cavity, making his roar significantly louder and more thunderous.

Lions hunt in packs and employ a strategy to drive their prey into a trap. The alpha lion positions himself on one side of a watering hole while the younger, stronger, and more dangerous members of the pack position themselves on the opposite side. When animals come to the watering hole, the alpha lion roars. The frightened animals instinctually react by running away from the sound of the roar and straight into the strongest, deadliest members of the pack.

Facing Our Fears in Sobriety

Similarly, we often reacted to fear by running away—and heading right into the arms of our addiction. Taking contrary action means engaging in the counterintuitive step of facing our fear. Instead of running away from negative stressors that scare us, we find ways to tolerate our feelings and make healthier, more functional choices.

For example, many of us react to fear by isolating. We disconnect from sober resources and slide back into old forms of coping—which ultimately means using. Practicing contrary actions teaches us to respond to fear with healthy, self-soothing coping techniques rather than reacting with old addictive behaviors.

Creating a Contrary Actions List

Contrary actions take many forms. What they share in common is doing the opposite (contra) of the old, reactive addictive tendency to run away from our feelings and use. Here are suggestions of some contrary actions with which to respond to fear when you get triggered.

- Call your sponsor or sober buddy (you might want to program the number on speed dial).
- If a location is triggering you, get to a safe and sober place (your home, the home of a friend, a sober location, any place you feel spiritually connected).
- Go to a 12-step meeting.
- Pray (third step, seventh step, Serenity Prayer, Prayer of St. Francis of Assisi).
- Meditate, journal.
- Physical exercise (make sure whatever exercise you do is fun)!
- Take a walk/hike, ride a bike, work in the garden or workshop, paint, sculpt, dance, cook a meal, bake a cake/pie/cookies, take a bath, take a nap, get a manicure/pedicure, have a therapeutic massage.
- Read a book, magazine, play or listen to music.

- Meet a friend for coffee.
- Clean your space.
- Do your laundry.
- Be of service to someone in need.
- Knit a sweater.
- Go to the movies.

Contrary Action List Exercise

List five contrary actions you can take when triggered. Be strategic here.

What is the best contrary action to take when—

I am home alone.

_____

_____

_____

At work.

_____

_____

_____

Unstructured free time.

_____

_____

_____

Driving in my car.

_____

_____

_____

Away from home on business or vacation.

_____

_____

_____

In the company of others who are drinking/using.

_____

_____

_____

Skill # 24 Putting It Together with a SOBER Action Plan

A SOBER action plan functions as an early warning system to protect our recovery. Like NORAD, an early warning system created by the United States to monitor threats against the country, we need to develop a SOBER system to detect when our sobriety is threatened.

Football players are trained to execute a preset series of plays without a huddle. This kind of predetermined action helps players perform well during high-stress situations. To do this, players practice this plan repeatedly until it becomes second nature.

Developing and Practicing Your Action Plan

I have adapted this principle to help you manage your recovery during times of high stress. There are five predetermined actions in a SOBER action plan:

STOP

OBSERVE

BREATHE (mindfulness)

EXECUTE CONTRARY ACTION

REGULATE/RECONNECT

Stop

We stop whatever we are doing when we feel ourselves engaging in negative thoughts, feelings, or sensations. The sooner we do this, the better. This can be as simple as noticing a thought, feeling, or bodily sensation that is uncomfortable. Simply take the time to stop what you are doing long enough to focus your attention on it.

Observe

Perform a scan on your thoughts, feelings, and sensations. What are you thinking? How does it feel in your body? What person, place, or thing might have triggered you? After a while, you will be able to associate certain sensations, like butterflies in your stomach, connected to feelings like fear or anxiety.

Observe where you are, who you are with, and what you are doing. Are you in a safe environment with people you trust? Are you engaging in a shady or sober activity? The truth is, virtually anything (negative or positive) can trigger the desire to use. Do not underestimate the "baffling, cunning, and powerful" nature of these triggers. We dismiss or ignore them at our peril.

Breathe

Begin diaphragmatic, mindful breathing, in and out through the nose. You can do this anywhere, with your eyes open, in a way that no one will be aware you are doing it. Check in with yourself. Notice what thoughts, feelings, sensations come up. Remember, you do not need to *do* anything. Simply continue to observe what is going on inside you. If it helps, name the sensations, thoughts, and feelings as they rise into consciousness.

(*I am feeling a twinge in my stomach. That happens when I become nervous. I can observe this nervous sensation float out of my consciousness.*)

Continue diaphragmatic breathing for at least sixty seconds. Your central nervous system (CNS) will automatically start to calm you and regulate your system and the trigger/trance will begin to subside.

Execute a Contrary Action

The moment we feel the trigger begin to subside and clarity return, we need to execute our preset contrary action. It is important to get into action! Do not hesitate. If we do not seize the moment of clarity, the trance state is likely to return and pull us back into the addictive cycle.

This is why it is so important to have a predetermined action you are prepared to set in motion without thinking. What contrary actions are you willing to implement?

- Call your sponsor/sober buddy/family member.
- Get away from the dangerous/slippery place immediately.
- Get to a place you feel safe.
- Recite a positive affirmation or prayer.
- Go for a run or exercise.
- Take a nap.
- Take a bath or shower.
- Get a massage/manicure.

List three contrary actions you can take immediately:

1.

2.

3.

Reconnect/Restore

Once you have taken action and the trigger has subsided, even temporarily, it is important that you reconnect with your sober support network. This enables you to restore a sense of balance and equilibrium so you can continue your day. Reconnecting and restoring serve a very important function. In addition to avoiding a slip, continuing with your recovery-based activities for the day strengthens the new sobriety circuits being created in your brain. (See chart below.)

Breaking the Addictive Cycle

The SOBER action plan not only breaks the addictive cycle; it creates a new sobriety cycle. This new pattern of behavior becomes stronger and stronger the more it is repeated. Each time you catch your trigger early enough to take a healthy, contrary action, you create and strengthen neural pathways for long-term sobriety, health, and wellness!

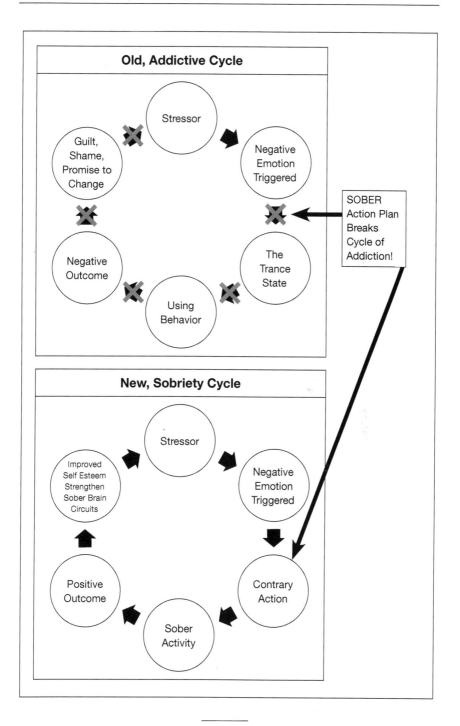

PART THREE

Mid Recovery

*Integrating Individual Staying Sober
Skills into a Balanced, Sober Lifestyle*

Chapter 9: Width in Recovery—Measuring the Quality of Sobriety

Chapter 10: Understanding the Spectrum of Sobriety (SOS)

Chapter 11: Using the SOS Checklist

Chapter 12: Creating a Day with the Staying Sober Recovery Planner

Width in Recovery— Measuring the Quality of Sobriety

In Mid Recovery, we expand the concept of measuring recovery beyond the one-dimensional view of sobriety as a function of time. The traditional view in the recovery community has been to equate the length of time you are abstinent with the quality of your recovery. The formula is something like this: length of sober time = quality of recovery.

In addition to the length of your sobriety (the number of days you have been clean/sober), Staying Sober will teach you how to measure the quality of your sobriety using the dimension of *width*.

The *width* of your recovery is determined by the number of sobriety-based skills/activities you engage in on a daily/weekly basis.

Traditional Way to Measure Sobriety—Length

The length of sobriety is measured by the number of consecutive days you abstain from drinking/drugging. This is an important and necessary measurement of recovery.

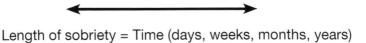

Length of sobriety = Time (days, weeks, months, years)

Width of Sobriety

In addition to the length of abstinence, I believe there is value in measuring the amount of time spent on a daily/weekly basis engaged in sobriety-centric behaviors and activities. The level of engagement in recovery is the *width* of recovery.

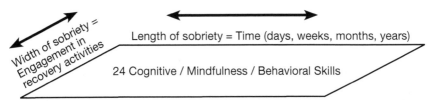

"Dry Drunk" Syndrome

Dry drunks are individuals who remain abstinent but do not actively engage in changing from addictive to recovery-based coping techniques. As a result, they tend to experience a lower quality of recovery. Even while they do not use, they continue to think, feel, and behave in addictive ways.

These people tend to engage in other self-defeating patterns of behavior about which they appear to have little insight. This creates ongoing distress. I think of this level of recovery as narrow and

difficult to maintain. Without the non-using coping tools to assist them, these individuals rely on sheer willpower to maintain their emotional balance and sobriety. It is difficult to maintain emotional balance, like walking a tightrope.

Dry drunks take many forms. Some present with ongoing symptoms of irritability and anger. They are like volcanoes that are perpetually on the verge of eruption. People tend to walk on eggshells around them for fear of setting off an explosion. Other dry drunks manifest symptoms of different addictive behavior, like overeating, compulsive shopping, gambling, or inappropriate sexual behavior. In both cases, these are individuals who don't use drugs/alcohol but retain their addictive mindset.

Width Creates Stability

The path of recovery is widened with ongoing engagement in sobriety-centric skills and activities. The greater the level of engagement with everyday life, the larger, more expansive, and stable the experience of sobriety will be for you. The width or level of engagement in sober activities broadens your recovery, giving it more variety, context, and strength. This makes the path of recovery easier to traverse, like walking on a well-maintained path.

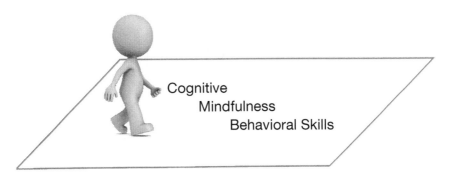

Cognitive
Mindfulness
Behavioral Skills

CHAPTER 10

Understanding the Spectrum of Sobriety (SOS)

Measuring the width of sobriety—the level of engagement in sobriety-centric activities—provides us with a fuller, more complete picture of our recovery. It gives us a valuable tool to measure and monitor our level of engagement in sobriety on a daily basis.

I have developed a spectrum along which to measure different levels of sobriety. The level of sobriety is determined by the number of sobriety-centric skills and activities (the 24 recovery skills) used each day.

Spectrum of Sobriety

Recovery	Maintenance	Lapse	Slip	Relapse	Collapse

Recovery: The most robust level of engagement. Individuals are attending meetings and implementing an average of ten or more sobriety-centric tools, skills, or activities on a daily basis.

Maintenance: This level of sobriety is also characterized by engaging in sobriety skills/activities every day. A regular schedule of meetings and recovery-centric activities are maintained, with occasional exceptions.

Lapse: Engagement in daily recovery begins to decrease. Feelings of being unmotivated or disengaged emerge. Meeting attendance is spotty. Use of recovery skills becomes irregular. Individuals are still abstinent, but not sober.

Slip: An initial using experience after a period of sobriety.

Relapse: The slip is hidden. The belief takes hold that individuals can use drugs or alcohol "responsibly." Over time, the using pattern returns to the pre-sobriety level.

Collapse: Sobriety is abandoned. A new bottom created with ever more devastating negative consequences.

Spectrum of Sobriety Checklist

The week of:	Mon	Tue	Wed	Thu	Fri	Sat	Sun
Skill #1: CBT							
Skill #2: Affirmations							
Skill #3: Attitude of Gratitude							
Skill #4: Read Daily Meditation							
Skill #5: Journaling							
Skill #6: Mindfulness Meditation							
Skill #7: Visualization							
Skill #8: Mapping Triggers with Body Scan							
Skill #9: The Power of Prayer							
Skill #10: Boundary Setting							
Skill #11: Sober Home/Work/School							
Skill #12: Personal Appearance/Hygiene							
Skill #13: Self-Soothing Behaviors							
Skill #14: Healthy Diet and Nutrition							
Skill #15: Attend Support Group Meetings/AA							
Skill #16: Sober Support Network							
Skill #17: Sober FUN!							
Skill #18: Active Listening							
Skill #19: Assertive Communications							
Skill #20: Dealing with Resentments							
Skill #21: Making Amends							
Skill #22: Bookending							
Skill #23: Take Contrary Actions							
Skill #24: SOBER Action Plan							
Total Daily Points							

SOS Point System

One (1) point for each daily activity.

Three (3) points for each meeting attended.

SOS Level	Daily	Weekly
Recovery	10 +	70 +
Maintenance	5 - 9	35-63
Lapsing	0 - 4	0 - 28

Make copies to track your progress!

CHAPTER 11

Using the SOS Checklist

Y̲ou can use the SOS checklist found in Chapter 10 to monitor your progress on a daily, weekly, or longer basis. The SOS checklist is also available in Excel format; download it for free at www.stayingsoberhandbook.com.

Input your weekly SOS point totals to track your progress over extended periods of time. You can also build reports to gather important information about your recovery. For example, are you more engaged in your recovery during the week than on weekends?

I also find the SOS checklist is a good way to keep your schedule in balance. For example, you might notice that your daily points drop below 4 (into the "Lapse" category) every Friday.

That might prompt you to rethink your schedule on Fridays. Have you overscheduled non-sobriety tasks on Fridays? Do you engage in high-stress activities on that day? Is a change in schedule indicated? The SOS checklist is a great information source about the quality of your sobriety.

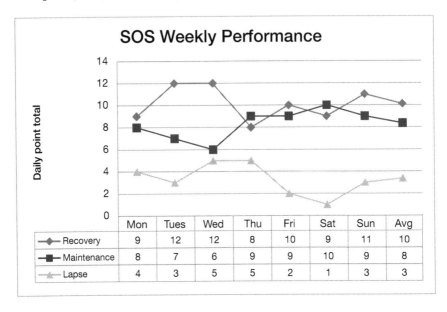

SOS Weekly Performance

	Mon	Tues	Wed	Thu	Fri	Sat	Sun	Avg
Recovery	9	12	12	8	10	9	11	10
Maintenance	8	7	6	9	9	10	9	8
Lapse	4	3	5	5	2	1	3	3

CHAPTER 12

Creating a Day with the Staying Sober Recovery Planner

Now that you understand how to measure the quality of your sobriety using the SOS checklist, the task becomes finding how to fit sobriety-centric activities into a balanced daily and weekly routine. The competing demands of life in sobriety can often be difficult to prioritize. How do you find the time for your recovery as well as your work, school, family, friends, shopping for food, doing the laundry, getting exercise, and fun?

Organizing Recovery One Day at a Time

Rome was not built in a day. The same applies to building a sober routine. It begins with creating a daily sober schedule that is balanced, manageable, and flexible enough to be consistently sustained over time.

To help organize your Early Recovery skills into a daily/weekly schedule that is balanced, dynamic, and easy to follow, I have created a simple daily organizer for you to use. On the left side are the hours of the day, broken into 30-minute segments. In the lower right are the 24 core sobriety skills you learned.

You can now plan how to stay at the recovery level by simply including enough sobriety skills in the course of the day.

Staying Sober Daily Planner			Date:	
Time	SOS Activity	Points	*Recovery may be hard by the yard, but it's a cinch by the inch!*	
6:00				
6:30			Today's *to-do* list	
7:00				
7:30				
8:00				
8:30				
9:00				
9:30				
10:00				
10:30				
11:00				
11:30				
12:00				
12:30				
1:00				
1:30				
2:00				
2:30				
3:00				
3:30			CBT—Mood log	**Spectrum of Sobriety**
4:00			Affirmations	
4:00			Attitude of Gratitude	**SOS Quality of Sobriety**
4:30			Read Daily Meditation	**Daily Point Total**
4:30			Journaling	is:_____
5:00			Mindfulness Meditation	
5:30			Visualization	**Today I am in**
5:30			Mapping Triggers with Body Scan	____Recovery
6:00			The Power of Prayer	____Maintenance
6:30			Boundary Setting	____Lapse
6:30			Create Sober Home/Work/School	
7:00			Personal Appearance and Hygiene	
7:30			Self-Soothing Behaviors	**Spectrum of Sobriety**
7:30			Healthy Diet and Nutrition	**Point System**
8:00			Sober Community / AA	
8:30			Build Sober Support Network	10 + Recovery
8:30			Sober FUN!	5-9 Maintenance
9:00			Active Listening	4 or less Lapse
9:30			Assertive Communications	
9:30			Dealing with Resentments	1 point per activity
10:00			Making Amends	3 points per meeting
10:30			Bookending	
10:30			Take Contrary Actions	
11:00			SOBER Action Plan	

Staying Sober Recovery Planner— An Example

The good news is that recovery-level sobriety is easy if you are willing to create a schedule and stick to it. To give you an idea, I have created a sample sobriety schedule in which you can accumulate ten or more points a day—nine of them before you even leave home in the morning!

Personal hygiene: Make your bed, straighten up your space, clean up after breakfast (3–5 minutes).

Healthy diet/nutrition: Eat a balanced, nutritious breakfast (15 minutes).

Serenity prayer: "God, grant me the serenity to accept the things I cannot change, the courage to change the things I can, and the wisdom to know the difference." I say this prayer as soon as I open my eyes (10 seconds).

Reading daily meditation: I can comfortably read the quote, two or three short paragraphs, and the call to action in about a minute and a half (90 seconds).

Writing a gratitude list: Many items on the list can be repeated. (I am grateful for my recovery, parents, sponsor, etc.) Try to add at least one new item, large or small, to your list every day. This keeps the daily exercise fresh (2–3 minutes).

Reciting affirmations: I like to rotate existing affirmations and create new ones based on what is going on in my life at the time (30 seconds).

Mindfulness practice: Listen to eight-minute guided meditation (8 minutes).

Attend 10 a.m. 12-step meeting.

Time	SOS Activity	Points
6:00		
6:30	Wake up, shower	
7:00	Shave, dress, groom	1
7:30	Healthy breakfast	1
8:00	Clean space/make bed	1
8:30	Serenity prayer, daily reading	2
9:00	Affirmation, gratitude, mindfulness	3
9:30		
10:00	Meeting	3
	Total Morning Points!	11

Staying Sober by Staying Consistent

Perhaps the biggest challenge in Mid Recovery, after creating a daily/weekly routine, is *sticking to it*. Being consistent over time is the key to recovery. This does not come naturally to many of us. In fact, most of us are notorious for making grand, sweeping plans to change—only to have them unravel after a week or so.

Under Commit, Over Deliver

It is better to schedule less and do more in the beginning. For example, if you schedule going to three meetings a week and actually attend four, you are way ahead of the game. If, on the other hand, you schedule four and only get to three of them, you set yourself up for failure. My advice is to play it smart by under committing and over delivering.

Habituating Sobriety

We are all creatures of habit. Behavioral scientists tell us that if we consciously repeat the same behavior for twenty-one days, we lay down a neuronal pathway we refer to as a "habit." The longer we repeat that behavior, the more deeply ingrained it becomes. Over time, our habits become so deeply ingrained that we no longer have to consciously think about them. They become second nature. The same is true with our recovery. The more consistent we are over time, the more natural and normal sobriety becomes.

Your Brain Is Still Healing

Feelings of boredom, frustration, and impatience are normal at this point. This is often the result of your body's healing process. While you were in addiction, you exhausted your ability to naturally produce self-soothing neurochemicals like dopamine, serotonin, gamma-aminobutyric acid (GABA), and oxytocin. Your brain needs time to become accustomed to producing these naturally occurring chemicals again.

Maintaining Balance

Perhaps the biggest challenge in Mid Recovery is integrating sobriety-centric practices into our lives in a balanced way. As addicts, we are accustomed to immediate gratification. Practicing delayed gratification and keeping our disposition on an even keel takes time, practice, and patience.

When we do not keep things in balance, we tend to revert to impulsive, emotionally charged decision making. This approach is seldom successful. It is easy for us to become impatient. We might set unrealistic goals and end up feeling overwhelmed, scared, and resentful. This sets us up for relapse.

It is analogous to people who join a gym and are determined to get results immediately. They set up unrealistic goals and push themselves to the limit during every workout. After a number of weeks of this, one of two things happens.

The **first** is that they have focused so much time and energy on working out that other parts of their life gets thrown out of balance. This creates stress and promotes burnout. Or second—and this is even more serious—they push themselves harder than is healthy and end up getting injured. Either way, they do not achieve their goal and they end up feeling more frustrated than before.

Learning Why Less Is More

The idea that we can get better results by doing less can seem counterintuitive. Our thinking typically goes along the lines of, "If one is good, three is better."

But building a balanced weekly routine requires the opposite approach. We take it slowly. We make sure that every time a stressful activity is added, we add a self-soothing one as well. Creating this kind of balanced, sober routine takes time, practice, and ongoing adjustments.

PART FOUR

Long-Term Recovery

Growth, Development, and Personal Transformation

Chapter 13: Maintenance and OnGoing Growth

Chapter 14: Depth in Recovery—The Process of Transformation

Chapter 15: Deepening Sobriety through Acts of Service

CHAPTER 13

Maintenance and Ongoing Growth

Long-Term Recovery is about ongoing growth and development, inside and out. On the inside, we come to terms with old, self-defeating patterns of behavior. On the outside, we continue to grow emotionally and financially, becoming stable, positive, productive members of our community.

As we continue to engage in the process of recovery, something transformational starts to happen. We begin to experience a new sense of self that is larger, deeper, and more connected. We experience waves of contentment, well-being, or peace of mind at unexpected moments.

We suddenly notice the beauty of a tree we walked past hundreds of times without ever noticing its calm majesty. We seem to intuit what others are going to say by the smallest gesture or look in their eye. Developing this sensitivity to the environment and to others is an aspect of *depth* in recovery

CHAPTER 14

Depth in Recovery—
The Process of Transformation

Returning to our multidimensional model, I invite you to consider a third dimension of recovery: *depth*. We began with *length* as the traditional way to measure sobriety (the number of days we have remained drug- or alcohol-free). Next, we learned about the *width* in recovery, which measures the quality of sobriety by the amount of drug-free time spent engaged in recovery-related activities.

The dimension of depth measures your ongoing engagement in recovery too, but in subtle, subjective ways. Depth is less bound by time or activity than by the internal transformation of personality traits and worldview.

This stage of development is also about deepening the quality of our sobriety in terms of our commitment to share it with others through acts of service and functioning as positive, productive members of our local community.

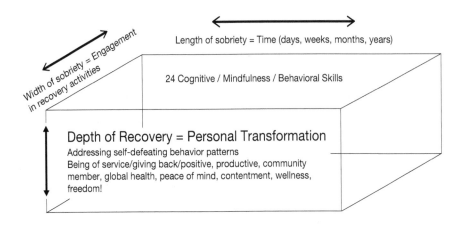

Length of sobriety = Time (days, weeks, months, years)

Width of sobriety = Engagement in recovery activities

24 Cognitive / Mindfulness / Behavioral Skills

Depth of Recovery = Personal Transformation
Addressing self-defeating behavior patterns
Being of service/giving back/positive, productive, community member, global health, peace of mind, contentment, wellness, freedom!

The Depth Experience

The art historian, Sir Kenneth Clark, once observed, "I cannot define civilization, but I know when I am in its presence." The same is true of the experience of depth. We might not have the words to describe exactly what depth in recovery is, but our internal experience is unmistakable.

One account of depth comes from a client who described himself as a "man of science." To this day he maintains his staunch position as an atheist.

One morning, while doing his mindfulness practice outdoors, he reported experiencing a wave of soothing, healing energy. He reported it swept up his body from his toes to the top of his head. The experience was palpable and like nothing he had ever felt before. He went on to describe the wave of healing as a form of light that seemed to pass through him, almost like an electrical current that entered through his toes and passed out through the top of his head. When it ended, my client reported a profound sense of clarity and "alive-ness." He described a heightened level of perception in which "everything was illuminated."

Another account of depth comes from a client who reported depth as an intimate moment of insight. This individual had been sober for a few years, but was haunted by the feeling that something was wrong. "I was waiting for people to find out I was a liar, a fake."

One evening, he arrived home after work before his wife. He decided to take their dog out for a walk. The cool, evening breeze felt great and he decided to extend his walk. When he approached his house at the end of the walk, he saw his wife's car parked in the driveway. That feeling of being "found out" returned. His stomach twisted into a knot of fear and anxiety. He remembered all the nights he came home late after drinking and scrambled to remember the lie he had told his wife earlier in the day. In a stunning shock of the obvious, he realized, "I don't have to have a good memory anymore. All I need to do is tell the truth!" The simplicity of this insight spoke volumes to this man about the depth of his personal growth and transformation.

CHAPTER 15

Deepening Sobriety through Acts of Service

One of the most important and least understood sobriety skills is being of service to others. The idea behind being of service is simple: help others with no expectation of reward. While the 12-step community embraced this idea early on, the tradition of service and selflessness can be traced back to the beginning of all faith and wisdom traditions. In my view, it is the glue that keeps communities together and gives life meaning beyond our selfish desires.

The Counterintuitive Nature of Giving

When active in our addiction, the idea of giving and getting nothing in return might seem counterintuitive. The nature of our disease left us in an ongoing state of deprivation and self-absorption We constantly felt the need for more. We were selfish, self-involved, and often did not take the needs of others into consideration. Being of service is an opportunity to reverse this addictive mindset.

Service is also a way to restore balance to our lives. When we first got sober, many people helped us, directly or indirectly. In the case of the 12-step community, we were made to feel welcomed and offered help at virtually every turn. Doing this for others is how we pay our debt of gratitude forward.

Being of Service

As the phrase suggests, service is a state of being, an attitude, a mindset, a positive approach to the way we show up in the world. When we cultivate a service mentality, we suddenly realize that every word we speak and each action we take is an opportunity to serve the common good. This can mean things as simple as smiling and saying hello in a friendly voice to people we pass in the street, holding the door open for others, picking up a piece of litter on the street, or calling someone in need of support.

From Selfishness to Selflessness

Prior to sobriety, the idea that "it is better to give than receive" was an empty platitude to me. I was quite selfish and cynical in my addiction. My thoughts on the matter were based on advice I had received from my father: "It is a jungle out there. You need to look out for yourself. The only question you should ask in any situation is, 'what's in it for me?'"

I learned that my selfishness only bred more selfishness. It separated me from others. I was lonely, distrustful, and scared most of the time. Learning to be of service to others is a precious gift of recovery that I now give myself every day. I feel great when I am of service to others.

Regardless of where you have come from—no matter your gender, ethnicity, age, culture, religion, health, or wealth—the importance of being of service is reflected back to us from every corner of the world.

Being of service is a deeply spiritual practice. I believe it is one of the things that makes us unique as a species. Human beings are not the strongest or the fastest creatures on the planet. I believe it is our capacity to look after one another and to live in supportive, interdependent communities that has enabled us to survive and ultimately thrive. I believe the same is true in our recovery communities. Our individual willingness to be of service to others is what keeps all of us sober. When we perform anonymous acts of service, amazing things happen!

Different Traditions, the Same Message

- He who performs one tiny act of kindness, heals the world. —*The Talmud*
- The best way to find yourself is to lose yourself in the service of others. —*Mahatma Gandhi*
- Among us, who is above must be in service of the others. This doesn't mean we have to wash each other's feet every day, but we must help one another. —*Pope Francis*
- A generous heart, kind speech, and a life of service and compassion are the things which renew humanity. —*Buddha*
- I slept and I dreamed that life is all joy. I woke and I saw that life is all service. I served and I saw that service is joy. —*Kahlil Gibran*
- You will not attain righteousness till you spend in charity of the things you love. —The Qur'an, Chapter 3, verse 92.

Being of Service—Exercise

What does being of service mean to me? How can I positively impact the lives of others with no expectation of reward? Make a list of 10 things you can do today to be of service. Remember, there is no act too small, be it holding the door open for someone, greeting a stranger with a friendly smile, or picking up a piece of paper and putting it in the trash.

1. _____

_____

2. _____

_____

3. _____

_____

4. _____

_____

5. _____

_____

6. _____

_____

7. _____

_____

8. _____

_____

9. _____

_____

10. _____

_____

PART FIVE

Challenges in Recovery

Getting Stuck in Recovery: How to Identify Challenges and Overcome Them

Chapter 16: Self-Defeating Behavior Patterns and How to Overcome Them

Chapter 17: Incomplete Recovery

Chapter 18: Post-Acute Withdrawal Symptoms (PAWS)

Chapter 19: Overcoming PAWS with PRINTS

Self-Defeating Behavior Patterns and How to Overcome Them

There are many self-limiting/self-defeating behavior patterns that interfere with our health and well-being. For our purposes, I will focus on self-defeating behavior patterns (SDBP) as they relate to sobriety. I have collected them into three general categories: anxiety-based, depression-based, and mixed/dependent-based. The fact that I have separated them does not mean that these patterns do not sometimes overlap or that an individual cannot engage in more than one of these patterns.

Anxiety-Based SDBPs

The Rebel/Scapegoat: Individuals with this pattern were often the subject of physical, emotional, verbal, or sexual abuse. The person

---

Factoid **Self-Defeating Behavior Patterns**

Persistent, maladaptive patterns of behavior, often developed in childhood, that are detrimental to the self. This can include being drawn into problematic situations or relationships or failing to accomplish tasks crucial to life objectives. Behavior patterns that occur frequently and interfere with you getting what you want in your life.

---

who has suffered feels a lack of physical connection and might be awkward with outward displays of affection to others. They are distrustful, wary, and fear failure and authority. They seek control by being oppositional and defiant. They also experience an ongoing desire to run away or escape.

The person with this pattern might have great difficulty developing intimate relationships. They suffer from a profound fear of betrayal. While using rebellion to release anxiety, they experience guilt, shame, and low self-esteem. Rebel/Scapegoats also might be willing to take the blame for ALL family problems, whether they are responsible or not.

Jokester/Clown: These individuals use humor to break the tension and discharge negative emotions at home or school. They are willing to sacrifice their health, safety, and self-esteem to get a laugh. They like being the center of attention. They use humor to disguise, distract, or discount feelings of depression, anxiety, fear, loss, and trauma.

In adulthood, Jokester/Clowns develop an unquenchable thirst for attention, acceptance, approval, and feeling connected with others. Their self-worth is determined by others. They have an external locus of control. There might be an ongoing preoccupation with social status, appearance, public acceptance, money, achievement, and approval.

Perfectionist/Judge: This pattern is often the product of harsh, judgmental households. These children set unreasonably high standards for themselves and are harshly critical of their own performance. They tend to be overachievers but often do not feel good about their level of performance.

The perfectionism tendency can become generalized in adulthood. They hold others to the same impossible standards they set for themselves. They judge others harshly and are hypercritical of all who do not meet their standards. They believe people must be held responsible for their behavior. They respond to mistakes with harsh punishment, anger, and intolerance. They can be seen as harsh, cruel, or incapable of empathy.

Emotional Volcano: This pattern is often associated with inconsistent or confused parenting, which might have included chaotic periods of intense connection followed by periods of instability, neglect, or punishment in early childhood. In this person's early life, "stuff just happens" without explanation.

As adults, Emotional Volcanoes obsessively worry about being hurt, abused, humiliated, or taken advantage of. Sometimes this presents as paranoid belief that all perceived threats are intentional and that people are out to screw them. They feel powerless and fated to "always get the raw end of the deal."

They have great difficulty maintaining emotional regulation and often explode with anger over seemingly small, insignificant issues. They might exhibit great difficulty self-regulating and regaining emotional equilibrium after an eruption. They also experience being overwhelmed, feeling "numb," and displaying no emotion.

Depression-Based SDBPs

Conformist/Compliant/Invisible: This pattern originates in emotionally detached homes filled with fear, secrets, and lies. In these homes, children are to be seen and not heard. There are often instances of failure, financial instability, or death.

In adulthood, the Conformist/Compliant/Invisible individual often feels a pervasive fear of failure, impending doom, and inability to cope. There is a belief that failure is inevitable and they are not up to the task. They present as highly risk adverse. There is a tendency to procrastinate and put things off. They are emotionally shut down and do not want to "rock the boat." They exhibit great difficulty expressing their feelings and connecting with or trusting others. They cope with stress by emotionally withdrawing, even disappearing. They also struggle making decisions.

The Cynic: The person with this self-defeating behavior pattern often grew up in a disengaged, shaming, blaming, and chaotic family. Promises were broken without explanation and trust was betrayed. Experiences of loss, parental neglect, or abuse were common. There was financial instability. The foundation for this behavior pattern often includes early childhood loss, (death of family member or pet), divorce, or catastrophic disruption.

In adulthood, the Cynic demonstrates unrelenting focus on negative aspects of life: pain, death, disease, scandal, dishonesty, and an impending sense of betrayal and doom. They might experience fear of intimacy and have trouble maintaining relationships. They are often preoccupied by fear of losing what they have and unwilling to try new things (for fear they will not work out). The Cynic might be a constant complainer who is plagued by indecision. They also tend to procrastinate and put things off.

Failure to Launch: Often associated with failure in the family system (job, health, relationship) and a situation where risk taking, independent thinking, and action were discouraged. They might have experienced emotional and/or material scarcity and could have suffered from lack of physical and emotional support or affection.

In adulthood, the Failure to Launch individual feels an overwhelming fear of failure. Risk is to be avoided at all costs. They often suffer from low self-esteem and believe they are unable to improve their circumstances. They have feelings of inadequacy and might have difficulty making decisions for themselves, as well as a fear of making a mistake and a tendency to procrastinate. They might have feelings of loneliness, hopelessness, and alienation.

Mixed/Dependency-Based SDBPs

Victim: Tend to grow up in households dominated by experiences of shame, blame, and ridicule. As children they internalized negative messages, like they are stupid, incompetent, or otherwise incapable of caring for themselves.

Victims show excessive neediness as adults. They often become enmeshed with those who are perceived as stronger or more capable. They are willing to sacrifice their own needs to maintain relationships with people they believe will "help them out" but are unwilling to take responsibility for their lives. Victims are procrastinators and excuse makers with ongoing emotional involvement in lives of others (often parents), at the expense of social development. They believe they cannot survive or be happy without the constant support of the other. They might also have feelings of being smothered by, or fused with, others. Victims also might be chronically ill and unable to care for themselves.

Caretaker/Rescuer: This pattern often develops as the result of being turned into a surrogate adult/parent by caregivers who are incapable to caring for themselves or others. This individual might believe that survival of the family is their responsibility, and their past might have involved caring for siblings and parents.

In adulthood, Caretaker/Rescuers focus on caring for the needs of others at the expense of caring for themselves. They create meaning in their lives by serving others and often feel empty inside. Over time, they grow depressed, resentful, and embittered that they are not appreciated. This is the model for codependency. They might experience great difficulty individuating self and often feel the need to control. They often have trouble creating an identity outside of the caretaker role and have difficulty setting and maintaining boundaries as well as letting go of resentments.

The Prince/Princess: People with this behavior pattern often grew up with excessive praise and attention accompanied by a lack of boundaries or structure. Children in these houses come to believe they are special and superior to others. They feel entitled to special rights and privileges because they believe they are exceptional (despite displaying few, if any, exceptional qualities) and are not subject to the same rules as everyone else.

In adulthood, the Prince/Princess might show an excessive sense of self-importance and the expectation that others will make sacrifices to meet their needs. They can also present as arrogant and selfish, and demonstrate a lack of empathy or concern for others.

Different Problems, Same Solution

Self-defeating behavior patterns follow the same cycle as addiction. Stressors trigger negative emotions and the need to avoid these feelings activates a trance-like state of denial. Old self-defeating behavior patterns can emerge as the new, addictive attempt to avoid negative feelings for a person in recovery. And like the addictive pattern, these self-defeating behaviors cause negative consequences and can lead to renewed feelings of hopelessness, guilt, and fear that nothing will ever change.

The solution to the cycle of SDBP is also the same as the SOBER action plan (described in Skill # 24.) The place to break the cycle is when we initially detect negative emotions in our body.

STOP

OBSERVE

BREATHE (mindfulness)

EXECUTE CONTRARY ACTION

REGULATE/RECONNECT

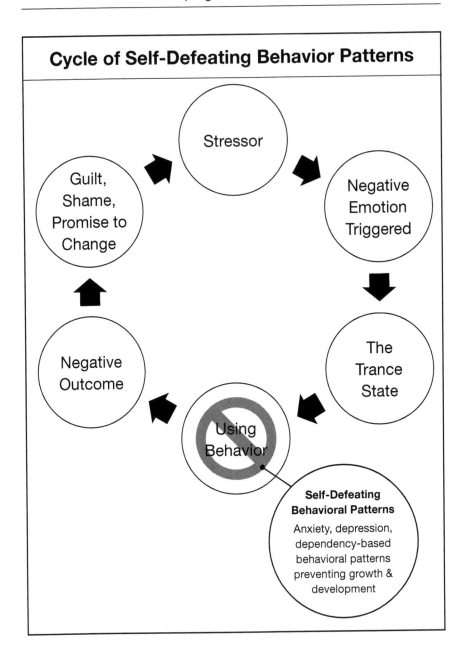

Cycle of Self-Defeating Behavior Patterns

Stressor

Negative Emotion Triggered

The Trance State

Using Behavior

Self-Defeating Behavioral Patterns

Anxiety, depression, dependency-based behavioral patterns preventing growth & development

Negative Outcome

Guilt, Shame, Promise to Change

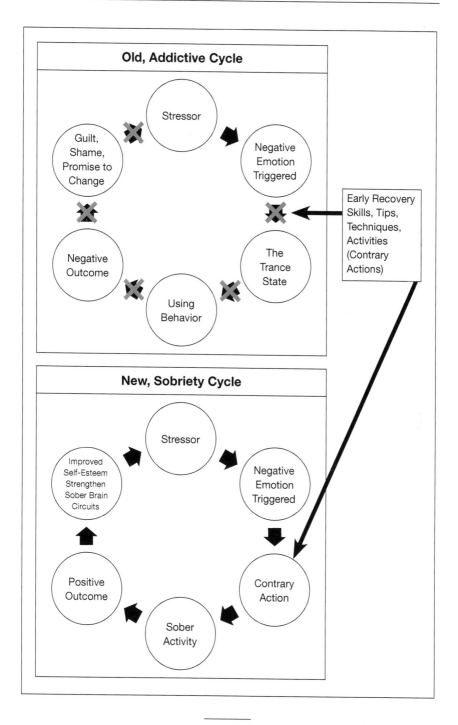

CHAPTER 17

Incomplete Recovery

Integrating Early Recovery tasks into a balanced, daily/weekly routine involves consistent change over time. Some changes are easier for us than others. Inevitably, we all get stuck somewhere along the way. For example, I found it easy to include daily meditation, affirmations, and a gratitude list into my daily routine. I did them first thing in the morning and I liked the way they made me feel.

Attending meetings in the evening was another matter. I was tired after work. I wanted to go home and veg out. Going to a meeting meant additional driving, the additional expense of eating out, and the increased anxiety of walking into a room full of strangers.

Underneath all of these activities was my fear of not being liked and accepted. I felt resentful that I needed to attend meetings when "everyone else got to go home and have a life!" As you can imagine, including meetings in my weekly routine was a challenge.

I found myself making excuses. There was too much traffic. I was too tired after a long day at work. It did not take long before mild/moderate symptoms of PAWS (Post Acute Withdrawal Symptoms—more on this in Chapter #18) set in. I became grouchy and resentful toward those who care about me. I started isolating and deepening into feelings of depression.

It was not until I was out of town at a friend's wedding that I actually felt the craving to drink resurface. The insanity of the disease came forward. I remember thinking, "Surely I can handle a sip of champagne to toast the bride and groom!" The seeming reasonableness of this thought got my attention. I had used the "I can handle having a sip on a special occasion" line. That thought made me realize how close I was to relapsing. I implemented my SOBER action plan and called my sponsor. He gave me great advice. Order a club soda for the toast, stay clear of the bar and people who are drunk, and make a graceful exit after the meal is served.

In ways I continue to find inexplicable, soon after I got off the phone I was approached by a man toting a similar glass of club soda and lime. He introduced himself and asked if I was in recovery! It turns out he was in recovery with twenty years of sobriety. We made plans to sit at the same table during the reception and supported each other. It has been my experience more times than I can remember that when I implement a recovery tool, I find allies of one form of another appear to support my recovery at just the right time and in just the right way.

The takeaway for me was that I was not growing in recovery because I was not including an important sobriety activity in my weekly routine. I noticed that by addressing my fears about going to meetings, I was able to change my perspective. I do not "have" to go to meetings. I "get" to go to meetings. Including this in my life is part of staying sober, healthy, and happy.

At some point in our growth and development, we all get stuck. The experience is one of frustration, boredom, feeling unmotivated, and having a sense of impatience in which we feel "we are going around in circles and nothing is changing."

This statement is half-right. The mastery of each developmental task is circular in nature. We practice the skill or task until we achieve mastery. Then we move on to the next sobriety skill. We all have long suits and short suits. That is why some tasks seem easier than others. It is not about being good or bad, smart or dumb, motivated or uncaring. It is about recognizing and accepting ourselves as we are.

It does not matter where we start in recovery. The important thing is that we engage in our recovery, no matter where we are. Once the healing process starts, it is only a matter of practice, consistency, and time before we accomplish even the most challenging of tasks.

I believe feeling stuck in recovery is actually a sign that important, challenging work is going on. I see it as the stress created when we grapple with deeply entrenched fears of not being good, capable, or entitled enough to overcome the challenge we are facing.

Stages of Incompletion: Repeating, Regressing, Relapsing

Working through these fears can temporarily stymie us. When this happen, it is important to remember that feeling stuck is only temporary. Getting unstuck is a process in which we often go through stages of incompleteness: repeating, regressing, and relapsing.

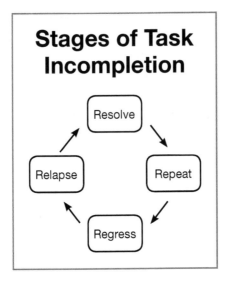

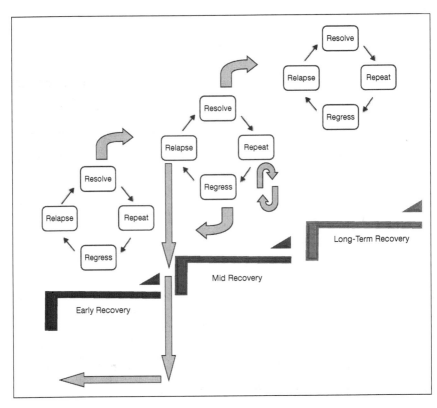

The Traffic Circle of Completeness

I visualize these stages of incompleteness as a traffic circle. We enter the traffic circle from a previous skill set, learn the new developmental task, and then exit the traffic circle and enter the next one. Some traffic circles take more than one trip around to complete. Sometimes it is necessary to regress to the previous traffic circle to reinforce an earlier skill set before returning to the current one. And sometimes, we relapse and need to reinitiate the entire process again from the beginning.

The important thing to remember is that we all get to define our own version of success and set our own pace. This is *your* sobriety. You get to take as much time as you need, and the only one you need to satisfy in this endeavor is you!

Repeating

One developmental task I needed to repeat was staying connected to others in my sober community. I found myself in a frustrating cycle of behavior that took a while to break. I complained to my sponsor that I felt left out and that no one in the AA community cared about me. It was suggested I get phone numbers from those people who expressly stated they would accept calls from people in the AA fellowship. I got two phone numbers and promised to call each of them once before the next meeting.

Days rolled by. I put off calling these two people. Fear and doubt surfaced immediately whenever I thought about completing this task. Automatic thoughts appeared out of nowhere. *They don't really want to hear from me. They only offered to take my call because they have to. What am I going to say, anyway? HI, I am calling because I don't like to call? The whole thing is stupid. I'll do it later.*

As I am sure you can guess, I did not make those two calls. In fact, I slipped even deeper into PAWS. In addition to the stress that surrounded calling others, I also felt stressed about having to face these people at the next meeting. My PAWS symptoms grew. I decided I could not go to the meeting and face these people. I felt ashamed. I was afraid my sponsor would judge me for "failing" to make the calls.

As a result, I regressed to old, addictive thinking. I could already feel resentment growing toward the entire fellowship. My decision making was clouded and impaired. The only thing that made "sense" in that deluded state of mind was to use (just to take the edge off and make me feel better.)

Suddenly, in the middle of this downward spiral, the phone rang. It was my sponsor inviting me to dinner. At dinner, I met up with other people in the fellowship. During the course of the meal, I told them what I was going through and listened as others told how they dealt with the same fear of calling. They shared how they addressed the issue.

Looking back, I realize how close I had come to relapsing. I also can see how easy it is for me to pick up the phone to connect with others in the program—a task I once felt was impossible for me to complete.

Regressing

For some, the experience of cycling/repeating and feeling stuck in recovery becomes increasingly distressful. It might reach the point where they suffer a kind of psychological or physical breakdown. Their lives become unmanageable. Something has to give.

This often shows up in the form of crisis. I once treated a young man who was living at home early in his sobriety. After nine months in recovery, he was clean, sober, and working. He consistently put away money toward getting his own place. He was working all aspects of his program, tracking his progress with his SOS checklist, attending meetings, and seeing to the rest of his obligations.

Working in consultation with me and others, he put together a sensible plan to move out of his parents' home and become more independent. He did his research and found a sober person looking for a roommate. They spent time together talking through all of the issues associated with becoming roommates. But the night before he was scheduled to move, *something happened*. He complained that his roommate had a dog. This was a deal breaker, as far as he was concerned. When asked whether this issue had come up before, he did not have much of an answer. He answered only that he "either forgot or did not think it was such a big deal until it was time to move."

A month later, he found another sober individual looking for a roommate. This time, he actually moved out of his parents' home and into an apartment. Three months later, however, he was back home, due to "issues" he had with the apartment building.

Self-Sabotage

This young man's issue was never about the dog or the apartment. Instead, the issue was a fear-driven negative core belief that he was not capable of caring for himself. Shortly after this second regression, he identified his fear and created a plan to overcome it. In the process, he also came to realize how this unresolved fear had found ways to sabotage his efforts to grow and develop. Once he learned how PAWS induced his regression from living independently to returning to his parent's home, he was able to move out. He has been living on his own now for several years.

Relapse

Relapses do not *just happen.* They are the end result of a long sequence of events that begin hours, days, weeks, or even months before you actually return to using drugs or alcohol. The process is activated by a stressor. Left untreated, the negative emotions triggered by the stressor show up as mild symptoms of PAWS. If these symptoms are discounted, dismissed, or denied, PAWS continues to grow and fester in the unconscious.

Emotions become erratic. There is a sense of internal lack of control. Concentration falters, thinking is impaired. You become emotionally dysregulated, either over- or under-reacting to normal situations. At this point, you become disenchanted with recovery. You create and cultivate resentments. You set up situations in which your options continue to narrow. Your sense of external control suffers. You become depressed and anxious. Your sleep and eating patterns suffer. You come to believe you have only two ways to end your pain and suffering: kill yourself or use.

The good news is that, at any point in this sequence, you can get the help you need to break the addictive cycle. All you need to do is ask. Staying Sober is judgment neutral regarding relapse. We are addicts. Sometimes addicts relapse.

My role is not to judge, but to treat. What is important is getting you the help you need. No matter how badly you might bottom out, or how many bridges you have burned, know that *there is always a way out of the madness.* You can get sober and stay sober.

I will never give up on you!

My only goal is finding a way to meet you wherever you are and to help you reinitiate the healing process. My experience has been, if you go to a 12-step meeting and ask those with long-term sobriety, most will tell you they repeated, regressed, or relapsed somewhere along the way.

CHAPTER 18

Post-Acute Withdrawal
Symptoms (PAWS)

There are no roses without thorns. —Spanish proverb

Changing from addictive to sobriety-based coping techniques and organizing them into a stable, balanced, ongoing daily/weekly routine is challenging. It requires implementing multiple levels of change (thinking, feeling, behavior) all at once. This process is sure to create stress and a longing to return to the familiar (though negative and self-defeating) status quo.

Substance abuse expert Terence Gorski collected the stress-related thoughts, feelings, and sensations that often become activated *after* the onset of sobriety and named them "Post-Acute Withdrawal Symptoms (PAWS)."

He distinguished PAWS from the acute withdrawal symptoms that accompany initial withdrawal and usually resolve in three to seven days. This time period can be longer in the case of withdrawal from certain drugs, such as benzodiazepines, methamphetamine, or methadone.

PAWS is a collection of physical, cognitive, emotional, and psychological symptoms that generally appear thirty to sixty days *after* the onset of abstinence. This delayed presentation might be attributed to the fresh, painful memories of the individual's hitting their most recent bottom.

After a month or two, when those negative memories begin to fade, PAWS begins to present. There is evidence to suggest that PAWS can grow in intensity from months three to six and then begin to subside and resolve in twelve to eighteen months.

It is important to know that PAWS is chronic in nature and can flare up months, years, or even decades after the onset of abstinence. NIDA speculates the long-term, chronic nature of PAWS might be due to structural changes caused by addiction that become embedded in neuronal pathways.

Major Symptoms of PAWS

Impaired thinking: Clear thinking and decision-making processes are impaired. It is difficult to concentrate, pay attention, and keep thoughts straight. There is an experience of fogginess or cloudy cognition.

Memory problems: Short-term memory problems are common, such as forgetting activities, commitments, and people's names. This might include losing keys, glasses, phone etc.

Emotional dysregulation: Over- or under-reacting to normal stressors. This can include "flying off the handle" and over-reacting to trivial matters, or experiencing numbness concerning highly emotional issues. In both cases, there is a sense of being out of control.

Sleep problems: Insomnia, including waking up in the middle of the night, not being able to get back to sleep, and having disturbing dreams. Excessive sleeping can also be seen as a symptom.

Impaired coordination or clumsiness: This symptom is often under-reported. It might include stumbling when walking or climbing stairs, bumping into furniture, balance issues, lack of eye-hand coordination, or accident-prone behavior.

Sensitivity to stress: Hypersensitivity to normal stressors and the inability to cope with stressful situations. It can also show up as a failure to maintain emotional equilibrium.

(From *Staying Sober,* Terence Gorski)

Additional Characteristics of PAWS

PAWS begins in the unconscious. Mild and moderate stages of PAWS remain below the level of conscious thought and might present as mild physical and emotional symptoms.

PAWS is progressive in nature. Unless symptoms are identified and addressed, they tend to build in strength and intensity.

PAWS is chronic. PAWS can appear long after the onset of sobriety.

PAWS and Relapse—Is There a Connection?

The delayed onset of PAWS might help explain why short-term, acute addiction treatment has such limited success. In most cases, intensive, thirty-day programs discharge clients *before* the symptoms of PAWS even begin to appear.

NIDA reports more than 60 percent of those who relapse within twelve months do so within three to six months of discharge. This relapse distribution appears to mirror the onset of PAWS.

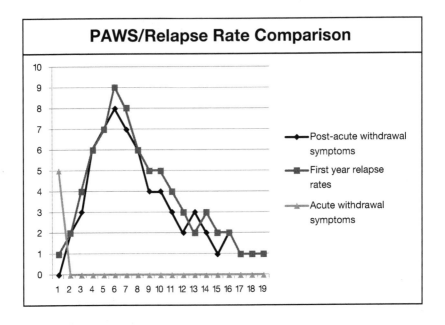

Dealing with Mild PAWS

Changing our daily and weekly routines from addictive to recovery-based activities creates stress. Most of us are not accustomed to taking on so much change at once. Stress-inducing changes tend to stir up old, negative core beliefs that reside below the level of consciousness.

The expression of this stress might initially show up as various forms of mild physical and emotional discomfort.

Physical Symptoms

- Tension or migraine headaches
- Neck aches, tightness in shoulders
- Tightness in the chest
- Butterflies or knots in the stomach
- Feeling on the verge of catching a cold

Emotional Symptoms

- Unexpected flashes of irritation
- Irrational fear
- Sudden lack of energy
- Sudden bouts of anxiety, a sense that "something is not right" despite all the positive developments in your life.

Cognitive Symptoms

- Odd, intrusive, or negative thoughts that appear out of nowhere
- Judgment/criticism of others
- Confusion, trouble making decisions, forgetfulness
- Intermittent periods of excessive worrying about self or others.
- Arrogance/complacency. "I will never use again, I got this."
- Focusing on or worrying about others instead of self
- Defensiveness
- Impulsive behaviors
- Loneliness/isolation

Connecting Symptoms to Circumstances

The intermittent nature of mild PAWS makes it easy to confuse with the normal stresses and strains of living "life on life's terms." If you are experiencing symptoms, see if you can attribute them to your current circumstances. If you recently experienced a breakup, job/career change, or moving, the chances are your stress level is connected to what is currently going on in your life.

On the other hand, if everything in your life appears to be going well and there are no obvious stressors present, these symptoms might be connected to PAWS.

Discounting, Dismissing, and Denying

When your inner emotional state does not match your outer circumstances, confusion and frustration often sets in. There is a nagging sense that things are not adding up or that something is wrong but you cannot figure out exactly what it is.

When presented with mild, internal discord that cannot be easily resolved, there is a natural tendency to discount, dismiss, or deny the importance of the symptoms. We often choose to focus on the outer circumstance of our lives and maintain a positive, recovery-centric attitude.

But when PAWS appears, I suggest you try "leaning into" the symptoms to get a better idea of what is going on. Do the thoughts, feelings, or sensations you are experiencing feel familiar? Do they have the same emotional resonance as your old, negative core beliefs, like "I'm damaged goods, unlovable, bad, or unworthy"?

If you suspect your symptoms are related to negative core beliefs, see if you can perform a CBT mood log in your head. What automatic thoughts come up about your current symptoms? What distortions are active? What kind of rational response can you come up with to restructure your thoughts to feel better?

Moderate PAWS

Denying the existence of distress actually adds an additional layer of stress on top of the existing symptoms. This new tension can merge with the original stressor and grow into a wider, more pervasive mood of discontent. This can become moderate PAWS. Symptoms include:

- Tunnel vision. You stop seeing yourself as a whole person, compartmentalizing instead. "If I can only solve this one problem, everything will be fine."

- Minor depression.
- Trouble thinking clearly and difficulty staying on task, concentrating.
- Loss of constructive planning. Your plans fail and you encounter setbacks.
- Emotional dysregulation (over/under reactions).
- Decision making suffers, often creating additional problems.
- Procrastination or trouble getting motivated.
- Feeling overwhelmed.
- Negative self-talk: "What's the use? I might as well give up. My plans aren't going to work out."
- Daydreaming or wishful thinking.
- Immature, regressive responses and behaviors.
- Easily angered or irritated with friends/others.
- Isolation.
- Commitment to recovery wavers until sobriety is no longer your first priority.

Internal Loss of Control

You lose the ability to control and redirect your thoughts/feelings. You become prone to mood swings, getting into funks that are difficult to understand or reverse. Symptoms of internal loss of control include:

- Increased clumsiness
- Self-pity
- Conscious lying
- Feeling trapped/having limited choices
- Unreasonable resentment
- Discontinuing treatment and AA completely

- Overwhelming isolation, frustration, anger
- Loss of behavioral control (thoughts, feelings, moods, and actions)

Getting a Case of the F*ck Its

One sign of moderate PAWS is suddenly feeling unmotivated, emotionally flat, or blah. Nothing seems fun or interesting. Your internal emotional landscape takes on a grayish, drab color.

This inner sense of emotional flatness can be particularly disorienting when you are actively engaged in your recovery in the outside world. You might also experience a disconnect between your inner emotional state and your outer, recovery-based activities.

A Stinkin' Thinkin' Monologue

This split between our outer and inner world can produce feelings of confusion and disappointment. One sign that this is happening to you is if you find yourself drifting into a stinkin' thinkin' monologue, which might sound like this:

Sobriety stinks! I am doing exactly what I've been told to do to stay sober. But instead of feeling better, I feel worse! I feel like I'm going crazy. I'm sober, I have a job, my life hasn't been this good in a long time. So why do I feel so antsy? Bored? It's like nothing is fun anymore. Most of the time, I feel tired, grouchy, or both.

I don't get it? I don't even know how to put it into words. When I feel like complaining, I don't know what to say. When I try to "act as if" I'm okay, I feel like a fake. I catch myself fantasizing about times when I used, just to take the edge off. Right now, I feel lousy ALL of the time. If this is what life in recovery is going to be like, I don't see the point. I might as well use and feel good some of the time!

BLACK FLAG Alert!

When you find yourself thinking along those lines, it is time to reach out for support! All you need to do is pick up the phone and tell someone you trust how you are feeling. Do not worry about your pride, or what others will say.

Remember, you *can't save your face and your butt at the same time!*

Severe PAWS

Left unchecked, moderate PAWS symptoms worsen. Recovery-centric thoughts, feelings, and behaviors break down. Irregular meeting attendance turns into non-attendance. There is a loss of structure and discipline. Feelings of depression, helplessness, and hopelessness set in. Other symptoms might include:

- Eating habits become irregular.
- Loss of motivation; the "f*ck its."
- Loss of daily structure and discipline.
- Periods of deep depression, hopelessness.
- Openly rejecting help, refusing feedback.

- Dissatisfaction with life; "everything sucks."
- Feeling powerless and scared.

External Loss of Control

The strength of PAWS can interfere with everyday functioning. You might feel unable to control your thoughts and emotions. Eventually, you become immobilized, unable to perform simple, daily tasks.

Emotional collapse: You emotionally bottom out. Life seems hopeless. You feel insane, irreparably broken, and filled with dread and despair. Breaking out of this unbearable state of pain appears limited to two choices: relapse or suicide.

Slip/relapse: A single using episode. You are at the crossroad. There is still an opportunity to call out the slip and get help.

Relapse: You keep the slip a secret and still do not ask for help. It is only a matter of time until the insanity of the disease takes over. Your behavior becomes unpredictable. You are soon using as much as you were before you got sober.

Collapse: The addictive cycle has you in its grip. You are in addictive freefall. A downward spiral of increasingly negative consequences piles new problems onto top of existing ones. Your life is out of control. You dig a deeper bottom of hopelessness and despair.

Cunning, Baffling, Powerful

When *The Big Book of AA* was written back in 1939, little was understood about the effect of addictive substances on the brain. At that time, alcoholism and addiction were thought to be bad habits engaged in by people of weak moral character or mental illness. AA was the first treatment protocol that described addiction as a disease for which there was no cure. AA also referred to the nature of alcoholism as "cunning, baffling, and powerful."

Biochemical Mood Signals

Since that time, we have learned an enormous amount about how drugs and alcohol affect the brain. New research and technology allow us to trace how the brain signals mild symptoms of PAWS below the level of conscious thought in the form of biochemicals that generate physical and emotional responses.

Interpreting the Signals

Mindfulness techniques give us the tools to monitor our bodies on a moment-to-moment basis. Our ability to focus awareness on bodily sensations enables us to identify early signals of PAWS *before* they break into consciousness as powerful cravings to use. This is an incredibly valuable skill. We now have a way to pick up and address these symptoms *before* they fester, grow, and surface as "cunning, baffling, and powerful" cravings to use.

Out of Sight Is Not Out of Mind

We ignore these early signs of PAWS at our peril. Just because we deny, discount, or ignore these symptoms, that does not make them go away. Left unaddressed, PAWS seems to cycle through the unconscious, growing in size, power, and intensity with each repetition.

Mild to moderate symptoms of PAWS can remain below the surface for days, weeks, months, or more. At some point, however PAWS becomes so powerful and pervasive that our distress breaks into consciousness, often with cyclonic force. This sudden and dramatic presentation makes it difficult to connect the symptoms to the original stressors. We are "baffled" about why we suddenly feel "powerful" cravings to use. Unable to figure out why this is, we often ascribe motives to the disease itself, and describe it as "cunning"— intentionally trying to regain control of us.

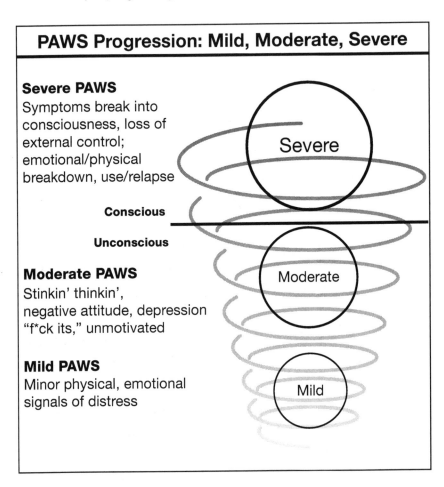

PAWS Progression: Mild, Moderate, Severe

Severe PAWS
Symptoms break into consciousness, loss of external control; emotional/physical breakdown, use/relapse

Severe

Conscious

Unconscious

Moderate PAWS
Stinkin' thinkin', negative attitude, depression "f*ck its," unmotivated

Moderate

Mild PAWS
Minor physical, emotional signals of distress

Mild

"While I am asleep in my bed at night,
my addiction is awake in the next room doing push-ups!"

CHAPTER 19

Overcoming PAWS with PRINTS

Staying sober requires us to change just about everything, from the way we think, feel, and behave to our routines, friends, and activities. Is it any wonder all of this change produces so much stress?

Stress triggers negative emotions and core beliefs that can activate the addictive cycle. To prevent this from happening, we need to monitor our stress level. Whenever we feel ourselves getting overwhelmed or feel PAWS-like symptoms appear, we need to activate our SOBER action plan. (More information about this plan appears at the end of PART TWO, Skill #24.)

Finding the Fear

Standing behind these negative core beliefs, in most cases, are childhood fears—fear of failure, rejection, abandonment, judgment, criticism, confrontation, physical/mental abuse, neglect, and ultimately death. These fears were terrifyingly real in early childhood. When reexamined in adulthood, we realize how inaccurate and irrational they are. But if this is true, why do we not simply use this logical approach and resolve these issues?

Breaking the Tether of Self-Limiting Beliefs

The reason is that we are not even conscious of these old, self-defeating beliefs. When circus trainers raise elephants, they start by tying one end of a clothesline around the baby elephant's leg and the other to a spike in the ground. When the baby elephant pulls against the tether and finds it cannot break free, it learns the clothesline is unbreakable and stops trying. This lesson is so deeply embedded in the mind of the animal that even when the elephant grows into adulthood and is capable of easily breaking free, it does not try. Why? Because the lesson learned in childhood has convinced this mammoth animal it is not possible. The same is true with us. We are held hostage by inaccurate, old, self-limiting beliefs.

The PAWS PRINT

A simple way to remember how to overcome PAWS is to think about making a PAWS PRINT. This is a five-step process you can use in addition to your SOBER action plan. It begins when you feel triggered to use—in other words, when the PAWS symptoms have become severe enough to break into a conscious desire to use.

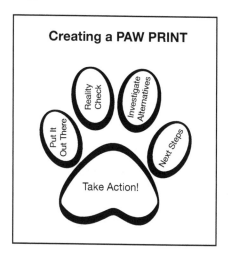

Creating a PAW PRINT

Put It Out There · Reality Check · Investigate Alternatives · Next Steps · Take Action!

Purge (or Put It Out There)

Reality Check

Investigate Alternatives

Next Steps

Take Action/Evaluate

First, implement your SOBER action plan to get safely out of the triggering situation and to reduce the intensity of the PAWS symptoms. Next, find a less stressful way to overcome the developmental challenge. I call this process creating a PAW PRINT, which has five steps: purge, reality check, investigate alternatives, next steps, and take action/evaluate.

Purge: When PAWS-induced stress gets you dysregulated and out of balance, it is important to just get these feelings off your chest. Do not worry about making sense. The important thing is to vent how you are feeling; to "put it out there." Ideally, this takes place in your support group where members know and care about you. A sober buddy or sponsor will do as a sounding board in a pinch.

Reality check: After you are done venting, ask for feedback. Often times, your presentation of details will come pouring out in such a jumble that others will ask clarifying questions. Be patient and answer them simply. Allow others to reflect back what they heard. It is very important to stay open minded and not get defensive.

Investigate alternatives: Out of this feedback, a number of alternative solutions often emerge. Brainstorm with others and allow yourself to consider a number of ways of overcoming your fear and addressing the challenge before you.

Next steps: Working in consultation with others, come up with a plan of action with which you are comfortable. Make a plan to accomplish your goal that is SMART: (specific, measurable, actionable and accountable, realistic, and time-bound).

Take action/evaluate: It's go time! Implement your plan. Do your best. Chances are certain things will work out better than others. There are always other factors that come into play that will require adjustments and fine tuning. Follow up and report all of this to your feedback group.

PART SIX

Guide to Family Healing

Promoting Family Healing, Addressing Outstanding Issues, and Creating New House Rules for Returning Loved Ones: Addiction Is a Family Disease That Affects Everyone

Chapter 20: The Addicted Family System

Chapter 21: Promoting Family Healing

Chapter 22: Codependence

Chapter 23: Codependence Self-Assessment

Chapter 24: Recovering from Codependence

Chapter 25: Setting Healthy Boundaries with Those in Recovery

Chapter 26: House Rules and Family Safety Plan

Chapter 27: Ending the Blame Game

Chapter 28: Creating a Family Genogram

The Addicted Family System

Happy families are all alike;
every unhappy family is unhappy in its own way. —Tolstoy

Families are perhaps our oldest and most enduring social system. They have been a source of protection and stability for as long as we have walked the earth. When the stability of the family system is threatened, its members instinctually adapt their behavior to defend and stabilize it.

Addiction represents a profound threat to the family system. As the disease progresses, the addicted family becomes less predictable, responsible, or accountable. The addict effectively stops participating and becomes a destabilizing influence on the status quo.

Other family members often react to this abdication of responsibility by picking up the slack. They adapt by trying to fill the vacuum. Over time, the roles of the healthy family members become stretched and distorted. These individuals experience increased stress, guilt, resentment, and shame. The family system closes ranks to keep the addiction a secret. Many times, the family unites around the struggle to deny the problem and attempt to appear "normal."

Addiction Is a Family Disease

It is easy to see the damage addiction causes to individuals. Their lives, careers, and relationships spin out of control. Less obvious, however, is the damage done to the family systems and its members.

No one is left unchanged by growing up in a family with addiction. The progressive nature of the disease incrementally distorts and dysregulates the family system. The rules, roles, and compensatory adaptations in addicted families tend to breed confusion, resentment, and shame.

Non-Addicted/Addicted Family System Comparison		
Family System Rules	Non-Addicted Family System	Addicted Family System
Needs of individual family members	Personal individuation supported by the family.	The centricity of the addict (their needs come first).
Communication	Communication is direct, clear, & specific.	Denial of addiction. Indirect communication, secrets, lies.
Safe to express emotions	Safe to express feelings openly, honestly.	Unsafe to express openly, honestly.
Family rules	Rules are dynamic, flexible, & responsive to change.	Rules are rigid, & unresponsive to change.
Connection to community/society	Family is open; many links to outside world.	Distrust of outsiders/ addiction kept secret at all cost.

The Impact of Addiction on Families

SAMHSA reports that each addict "profoundly impacts the lives of at least four other people, usually people who are closest to them." In 2013, the Centers for Disease Control and Prevention

(CDC) estimated there were thirty-five million people, over the age of eighteen, who met the criteria for addiction.

Taken together, these numbers suggest that approximately 140 million Americans (almost half the total US population) has been profoundly affected by the disease of addiction.

Roles in Addicted Family Systems

The Addict: Gripped by contradictions, life is out of control, highly sensitive, selfish, self-centered. Often charming, charismatic, talented. Irresponsible, dishonest, riddled with guilt, self-loathing.

Family Manager/Chief Enabler: Often spouse, partner of addict. Tend to over-function to compensate for addict's abdication of responsibility. Alternates between frustration/resentment and fear/anxiety as addiction deepens. Tries to cover up, deny addict's behavior, to "look good" to outsiders. Constantly feels overwhelmed, underappreciated, and on the verge of collapse.

The Hero: Seeks approval by excelling in school, athletics, making money. Family refers to him or her as the "star." Feels need to vindicate, redeem family from shame of addiction. Can suffer from low self-esteem; feels their value/worth is determined by what they do, not who they are.

The Rebel/Scapegoat: This family member tends to take the blame for everything. Engages in oppositional, high-risk, irresponsible behavior, negative attention seeking.

The Lost Child: This member adapts by retreating into a fantasy world, staying out of trouble and out of sight. Though they appear to be self-sufficient, they tend to be lonely, distrustful, and vulnerable to addiction.

Mascot/Jokester: Seeks to diffuse stress by joking, providing comic relief. Attracts positive attention with amusing, non-threatening behavior and distracts everyone from problems at hand. Often hyperactive with a short attention span. Main coping mechanism is laughter.

Healing Begins When Denial Ends

Most addicted family systems carry a deeply held belief that addiction is a source of shame and must be kept secret at all costs. Along with shame, there also can be feelings of guilt and the belief that family members are somehow responsible for the addiction.

Denying the Elephant in the Room

The shame, guilt, and anxiety about addiction are so painful, that the family system lapses into a state of denial as a coping mechanism. This creates an open secret in the center of the family, something everyone is aware of, but no one talks about.

This problem gets bigger and more problematic as the addict's behavior spins further and further out of control. Life takes on an air of unreality as excuses continue to be made to cover up for increasingly negative consequences.

Living this lie takes a great psychological toll on all family members. Confusion and anxiety give way to resentment and blame. Instead of uniting as a unit to get the addict help, the family splits into factions, each one blaming the other while the problem worsens. This is often referred to as the absurdity of having an "elephant in the room" that no one is willing to acknowledge.

CHAPTER 21

Promoting Family Healing

Family healing begins when you break the addictive code of silence. As soon as family members begin talking about the problem with one another and in support groups, the family starts to recover.

Educate Yourself

Addiction thrives in families that engage in secrets, lies, and denial. Healing begins when families educate themselves about how to make positive changes. There are organizations and fellowships specifically designed to educate and support you as you learn to communicate openly and honestly about the disease of addiction.

End Enabling Behavior

Enabling behavior refers to misguided attempts to "help" the addicts by shielding them from the negative consequences of their actions. Instead of helping them, enabling behavior does just the opposite. When you assist or collude with addicts to avoid them having to take responsibility for their actions, you actually prolong the addict's suffering by *enabling* them to continue their self-destructive behavior. As counterintuitive as it seems in the moment, the best thing to do is to stop enabling and force the addicts to face the consequences of their actions.

Treatment for All Family Members

Addiction affects everyone in the family system. And just as the addict requires treatment to get better, so do all the other family members. The family system has been stretched and distorted until it has become dysfunctional. Treatment is the best way to restore the family system to health.

All family members need an opportunity to process and resolve unspoken feelings of fear, guilt, resentment, anxiety, and shame. Secrets and lies need to be talked about openly in order for the family to heal. Attending individual and family therapy provides an opportunity to get things off your chest and feel better. The amount of time and effort spent attending therapy varies. I strongly recommend ALL family members attend at least two individual and two family sessions before deciding whether the process is worthwhile.

CHAPTER 22

Codependence

Codependence and enabling are different. Enabling is a specific behavior. Codependence is a personality type in which an individual displays enabling behavior as well as many other characteristics. Codependent individuals are unable to set boundaries. They display excessive reliance on other people for approval and might engage in dishonest, manipulative behavior. They tend to live in a perpetual state of crisis.

Codependency often begins as a coping mechanism for those who grow up in families with addiction, trauma, sickness, death, or chaos. The fear of rupture in the family system is so great that some members adapt by sacrificing their own needs and desires to please others and stabilize the family system.

Short-Term Benefits

In the short run, this codependent strategy—self-sacrifice to create stability—can be effective. The person develops the ability to:

- Survive in a crisis.
- Get by with little or no support.
- Split off terrifying feelings.
- Look after others.
- Create stability with controlling, manipulative behavior.

Long-Term Problems

- Intense, unstable interpersonal relationships.
- Inability to tolerate being alone, which is often accompanied by frantic efforts to avoid being alone.
- Chronic feelings of boredom and emptiness.
- Subordinating one's own needs to those of the person with whom they are involved.
- Overwhelming need for acceptance and approval.
- External locus of control (the belief that outside factors, beyond their control determine the course of their life).
- Engaging in dishonest, secretive, manipulative behavior.
- Living in a state of denial.
- Lacking an identity/sense of self separate from others; low self-worth.

CHAPTER 23

Codependence Self-Assessment

1. Did you ever lose time from work due to your relationship with an addicted person?

Yes   No

2. Have your relationships ever made your life unhappy?

Yes   No

3. Have your relationships ever affected your reputation?

Yes   No

4. Have you ever felt remorse after manipulating a situation?

Yes   No

5. Did you ever control situations to get money to pay debts or household bills or to otherwise solve financial difficulties that belong to someone else?

Yes   No

6. Has your involvement in a relationship caused a decrease in your personal ambition or efficiency?

Yes No

7. After a fight or disagreement, have you ever felt you must "get even"?

Yes No

8. After winning an argument, have you ever had a strong urge to restate your point?

Yes No

9. Did you often stay in a relationship until your last hope was gone?

Yes No

10. Did you ever borrow money to finance another person's addiction or associated crisis?

Yes No

11. Have you ever sold anything to finance another person's addiction or associated crisis?

Yes No

12. Were you ever reluctant to purchase necessary items because it might cause a disagreement?

Yes No

13. Did your relationships ever make you care less for your welfare or that of your family?

Yes No

14. Did you ever stay in a degrading or dangerous situation longer than you planned?

Yes No

15. Have you ever dragged old hurts into discussions about current items?

> Yes   No

16. Have you ever committed, or considered committing, an illegal act to finance someone's addiction?

> Yes   No

17. Did your relationships cause you to have difficulty in sleeping?

> Yes   No

18. Did arguments, disappointments, or frustrations ever create within you an urge to change someone else?

> Yes   No

19. Did you ever have an idea that if loved ones would only see things your way, life would be much better?

> Yes   No

20. Have you ever considered self-destructive acts (such as suicide or self-harm) as a result of your reactions or relationships?

> Yes   No

Answering yes to five or more of these questions is an indication that codependency has become a problem in your life.

CHAPTER 24

Recovering from Codependence

Recovering from codependent relationships is about separating your feelings for the addicts from their self-destructive behavior. Learning how to uncouple, or detach, your love for the individual from his or her addictive behavior is an extremely important skill to develop for a number of reasons.

The instinctual need for family members to restore the status quo by filling the vacuum left by the addict changes the relationships among all family members. In effect, the adaptations made by the rest of the family system (to pick up the slack) turn out to be a form of collusion, or co-addiction. Detaching from, or adapting your behavior so as not to take on responsibility for the addict's behavior and its consequences accomplishes two important goals:

1. It restores healthy boundaries among and between members of the system. It unites the non-addicted members in the family and creates positive pressure on the addict to seek help.

2. It directs non-addicted family members to take responsibility for their own behavior and to keep the focus on themselves. By "staying in their own lane," family members avoid the co-addictive tendency of trying to change or control the addict's behavior.

Detaching with Love

Detaching from an addict might sound easy, but it can be challenging to implement. It takes time, practice, and support to change codependent behavior. The important thing to remember is that your recovery comes first! Here are some tips to help promote your healing:

Surround yourself with external support. If you are struggling to understand someone you love or having trouble dealing with his or her actions, it is essential to have some support outside of your home environment. Find a close friend or a therapist with whom you can talk.

Remember that you are powerless over others. This is such an important thing to remember if you want to improve your relationships (or just live a positive life in general). No matter what you would like to believe, you have zero control over others. Realize this and you will free yourself from a lot of mental anguish.

Focus on the positives of the addict. If you are struggling with resentments toward the addict, take a moment and focus instead on the things you like/love/admire about that person.

Focus on positives about yourself. It is easy to get caught up in the negativity and chaos of the addict. It is important for the codependent person to detach from that negativity and focus on his or her own positive aspects: strength, resilience, and tenacity.

Remember who you are. There are times we get so enmeshed in the addict's affairs that we lose track of who and what we are. We need to set and maintain boundaries to prevent this from happening. Only by separating ourselves from the addict are we able to stay mindful of who we are.

The preflight instructions given before every plane flight include the direction for the adult to take care of themselves before helping others: "In the event the cabin loses air pressure, parents must put on their oxygen masks before helping children to put on theirs."

The same is true for the addict's partner or loved one. You must be healthy in order to help them get healthy.

Additional Resources

Individual therapy: Therapy can be extremely effective in teaching you how to "stay in your lane" and focus on your needs, rather than someone else.

Support groups and organizations: Groups like Al-Anon, AlaTeen, and CoDA (Co-Dependents Anonymous) are devoted to helping people heal from codependency.

Educational resources: Organizations like SAMHSA and NIDA are clearinghouses for literature, lectures, and other helpful resources to promote healing from codependency. A list of excellent books on the subject can be found in the Referrals and Resources section at the back of this book.

CHAPTER 25

Setting Healthy Boundaries with Those in Recovery

Boundaries define who we are. They mark the place "where I end and you begin." These demarcations are blurred or nonexistent in most addicted family systems. Boundaries help us determine what our responsibilities are and what they are not. We can only change ourselves, so boundaries help us define which things we can change and what we need to let go of and accept.

Types of Boundaries

Relational Boundaries

These boundaries are defined by the nature of our relationships. We have many types of relationships, each with its own boundaries. For example, giving an individual a hug and a kiss might be appropriate behavior when greeting a family member, but not with an employer or employee because the boundary governing affectionate behavior is different in those two situations. While some boundaries are common sense or dictated by culture, great care and communication is required to establish what is appropriate to both parties in all relationships.

Emotional Boundaries

Emotional boundaries are about the level of trust and intimacy you have in your relationships. These levels differ, depending on the person, your personal history with them, and other factors. These boundaries are dynamic; they can and do change and evolve over time. Determining who to share information with is often based on trust and intuition. There are no hard-and-fast rules. I find it best to go with your gut when deciding what to share with whom.

Physical Boundaries

Setting physical boundaries is about "safety first." The best way to establish appropriate physical boundaries is to communicate them clearly and openly. Any violation of your physical boundary is a serious matter and needs to be addressed firmly as soon as it occurs. It is always best for others to know where you stand.

Spiritual Boundaries

Spiritual boundaries define what we believe about our connections with others and the world around us. These boundaries include deeply held views about how we should treat others and how they should treat us in return.

People violate our spiritual boundaries when they attempt to control us by means of deceptive or manipulative spiritual/ethical beliefs. A cynical example of this is the recruitment of suicide bombers. Naïve, young men and women are manipulated into believing that blowing themselves up and killing others is part of their religious tradition and will earn them a special place in the afterlife.

Sexual Boundaries

Boundaries in this area bring together physical, emotional, and safety issues. Each individual determines his or her own sexual boundaries, based on gender, age, culture, ethics, and past experiences. Establishing firm, safe boundaries in this area is particularly important for those who have had their sexual boundaries violated earlier in life.

Financial Boundaries

You must know where you stand financially and what you are comfortable sharing or lending others. DO NOT say yes when you mean no! Maintaining this boundary can be a challenge for some at first. If you have established a boundary that you will not lend your money/car/stuff to anyone active in his or her addiction, you need to communicate it clearly.

Untreated addicts tend to be selfish and manipulative when it comes to getting what they want. The chances are good they will test your boundaries. Do not underestimate the imagination or tenacity of the addict. If they see you as the means to getting high (in the form of money, car, a ride, etc.), addicts are capable of saying or doing almost anything.

It is best in these situations to simply, directly refuse the request by saying "No." There is no need for lengthy explanations or excuses. If the addict begins to plead or otherwise manipulate you into conversation about the request, it is important NOT TO

ENGAGE. Instead, you can simply restate. "Is there something you do not understand about my response? The answer is no. Please do not ask me again."

Create a SOBER Action Plan for Boundaries

Stating and defending boundaries is challenging. You might find yourself slipping back into old behavior. Creating a SOBER action plan for codependent behavior is a good way to prevent this type of backsliding. This plan relies on the same SOBER action plan used by addicts to manage their recovery. (See PART TWO, Skill # 24.)

Stop. When you feel triggered by the addict to engage in codependent behavior, stop whatever you are saying or doing. Even if you are in the middle of a sentence, stop and say, "Excuse me. I need a minute."

Observe. How do you feel? Ask yourself if you are comfortable with the request being made. Does it violate, dismiss, or otherwise ignore/discount your boundary?

Breathe. Take slow, easy diaphragmatic breaths through your nose to clear your mind. After five to ten breaths, your nervous system will naturally reset itself. Triggering sensations (that is, codependent feelings of anxiety, fear, and disorientation) will subside.

Execute a contrary action. This is a predetermined response to make a healthy choice in any situation. It might be as simple as saying,

> "I am working on my codependency issues. One of my boundaries is not lending or giving money without thinking it over first. I will get back to you later." (You decide how much

time you need. An hour? An afternoon? After a good night's sleep? Take your time and don't allow them to rush you!)

Reconnect/Resume. After you make that statement, move on. Nothing else needs to be said on your part. Resume your activity or conversation where you left off.

Expect push-back. This new behavior/boundary might be tested at first, to see if you are serious. This might come in the form of repeating the request, pleading, or manipulative behavior.

Defending Your Boundaries

Addicts are likely to challenge your new boundaries. They do not do this to be malicious or with evil intent. This is the behavior of a sick person in the throes of their disease. Do not take it personally. A good strategy to fend off attempts to violate your boundaries is the, "When you, I feel, I need" technique described in the section on "Skill # 19 Assertive Communications."

In the example of a person with addiction asking you for money, even after you refuse, it might look like this:

When you . . . continue to ask me for money after I said no,

I feel . . . you are trying to manipulate me into violating my financial boundaries.

I need . . . to set boundaries to recover from codependent behavior. What I need from you is to honor these boundaries so I can have a healthier relationship with you and others.

A Boundary Defense Exercise

Think back to a recent time in which you felt your boundaries were being threatened—a person active in their addiction asks to borrow money "for an emergency," wants a ride to get to a "very important appointment," or needs to spend a night or two at your home on a "temporary basis." Now, create a defense of your boundary using this technique.

When you . . . _____

_____

I feel . . . _____

_____

I need . . . _____

_____

CHAPTER 26

Houses Rules and Family Safety Plan

Maintaining a safe, drug-free environment is important for addicts. Great care must be taken to determine appropriate boundaries in this area. Are non-addicted family members willing to refrain from drinking and/or storing alcohol in the house? The same question must be asked of family members who responsibly take pain medication (opiates) or antianxiety (benzodiazepines) medication. There are no hard-and-fast rules in this area, other than promoting the willingness of all family members to meet and problem solve together.

Hold Family Meetings

Establish a mutually agreed-upon day and time for all family members to get together for about an hour. This can be scheduled weekly, monthly, or on an as-needed basis. Attendance at family meetings is mandatory, but should not be made onerous. One sensible approach is to meet when you all share a meal together.

Establish guidelines: Family meetings run smoothly when everyone knows the rules and feels included. Some matters can be decided by a majority vote. Others might require unanimous agreement. Still others might be decided by the parent(s).

Everyone participates: Everyone who wants to will get an opportunity to express their views; however, only one person can speak at a time.

Respect given is respect earned: All family members are entitled to be treated with dignity and respect. Avoid shaming, blaming, shouting, or criticizing one another.

Keep it light and polite: If there are issues that cannot be resolved after five to ten minutes, table the issue and take it up with your therapist(s) or in smaller groups after the meeting is over.

Creating Family Safety Plan

A family safety plan is an agreement among all family members that sets clear, firm boundaries about how to support the addict in healthy, non-enabling ways. The plan spells out, step by step, what to do in the event the addict relapses or slips back into addictive or criminal behavior. The sole purpose of this plan is to keep the family safe and make sure the addict receives the help he or she needs as soon as possible.

Keep It Simple and Enforceable

Here are some guidelines to help you create a family safety plan:
1. Begin with a brief statement about the purpose of the plan.
2. Keep language clear and nonjudgmental.
3. Create graduated action steps (from mild to severe).
4. Have all family members agree to and sign the plan.
5. Post the plan in plain view of the family.

Additional Tips

- If an action step includes attending inpatient or outpatient treatment, mention it by name. Find out who to contact at the facility and how quickly the facility can accept your loved one in the event of a slip.

- Avoid using shaming, blaming language in the plan. Remember, the addict is not a bad person in need of punishment, but rather a sick person in need of treatment.

- If the addict's behavior results in destructive, dishonest behavior, they must be held accountable. The initial focus, however, must be on getting the addict the help they need. Addressing the consequences of their behavior can begin once they have been stabilized at the appropriate level of care.

- Ideally, the entire family should participate in drafting the plan. In the case of younger children, this can be in the form of a discussion or explanation. The addict should also be allowed to have input into the family safety plan and should agree (in writing) to follow the plan without hesitation or excuse.

A Sample Family Safety Plan

The purpose of this plan is to support your recovery as well as keep our family from slipping back into enabling behavior. We love you. We will never give up on you. We know you can stay sober and we will do all we can to support your sobriety.

In the past, we have attempted to help you in ways that actually enabled your addictive behavior to continue. We now understand that shielding you from the consequences of your actions actually prolonged your suffering. This family safety plan is set up to keep us all accountable for our actions and to promote mutual sobriety, health, and wellness.

We recognize addiction is a chronic disease that requires ongoing management and monitoring. We are also aware that only you can maintain your sobriety. You are responsible for following all aspects of your aftercare plan. We will support you when we can, but it is your job to get to meetings, therapy, and other recovery-related activities on your own.

Here is what we expect:

1. You will be drug tested, both scheduled and random. Refusal to submit to a test will be interpreted as an admission of drug use.

2. Your room, car, and possessions may be subject to search if we suspect drug use or behavior. Refusal to submit to a search will also be interpreted as an admission of drug use.

3. In the event of a slip, relapse, possession of drugs, or engaging in addictive behavior that puts the family at risk, you agree to the following actions:

   A. Increased attendance at AA or 12-step groups.

   B. Engagement (increased engagement) in individual therapy.

   C. Attend/complete outpatient treatment at (program name).

4. If using behavior continues:

   D. Move out of house

   E. Enter a sober living facility

   F. Attend/complete inpatient treatment at (program name)

I agree to all of the above.

_____

Signed and dated

Additional Family Safety issues

Is the addict in your family complying with the terms of the family safety plan? You might be on the lookout for subtle signs that drug or alcohol abuse has resumed or is continuing. Here are a series of issues that commonly come up in addicted family systems.

Question: *How do I know if my child is experimenting, using, or abusing drugs/alcohol?*

Physical and Health Warning Signs of Drug Abuse
- Bloodshot eyes or pupils that are smaller or larger than normal
- Frequent nosebleeds (might be associated with meth or cocaine)
- Changes in appetite or sleep patterns or sudden weight loss/gain
- Seizures without a history of epilepsy
- Deterioration in personal grooming or physical appearance
- Impaired coordination, injuries/accidents for which they can't or won't provide an explanation
- Unusual smells on breath, body, or clothing
- Shakes, tremors, incoherent or slurred speech, impaired or unstable coordination

Behavioral Signs of Alcohol or Drug Abuse
- Skipping class, declining grades, getting in trouble at school
- Drop in attendance and performance at work—loss of interest in activities, hobbies, sports or exercise—decreased motivation
- Complaints from coworkers, supervisors, teachers, or classmates
- Missing money, valuables, prescription drugs, borrowing and/or stealing money
- Acting isolated, silent, withdrawn, engaging in secretive or suspicious behaviors

- Clashes with family values and beliefs
- Preoccupation with alcohol and drug-related lifestyle in music, clothing, and posters
- Demanding more privacy, locking doors, avoiding eye contact
- Sudden change in relationships, friends, hangouts, and hobbies
- Frequently getting into trouble (arguments, fights, accidents, illegal activities)
- Using incense, perfume, air freshener to hide smell of smoke or drugs
- Using eye drops to mask bloodshot eyes and dilated pupils

Psychological Warning Signs of Alcohol or Drug Abuse

- Unexplained, confusing change in personality and/or attitude
- Sudden mood changes, irritability, angry outbursts, or laughing at nothing
- Periods of unusual hyperactivity or agitation
- Lack of motivation; inability to focus, appears lethargic or "spaced out"
- Appears fearful, withdrawn, anxious, or paranoid, with no apparent reason

(From the National Council on Alcoholism and Drug Dependence website)

Question: *If I suspect my child is using, should I search his or her room, phone, or social media sites?*

There is no "right" answer to this question. Here are some things to keep in mind. The most important thing to do, if you suspect drug use, is to keep the lines of communication open. Ask about the extent of drug use going on at their school. Ask whether they have experimented with any drugs (make sure you ask in nonjudgmental way). The best-case scenario is that your child feels safe enough to speak openly and honestly.

If your child denies drug/alcohol use and you are still suspicious, I suggest you watch and wait, and maybe ask a second time. You want to make clear to your child that maintaining an open, trusting relationship is more important to you than whether they are experimenting with drugs.

If they deny using on two occasions and you still suspect they are using, you might want to search their room, belongings, backpack, car, etc. Other places to look include dresser drawers, desk drawers, the glove compartment of the car, the back of closets, corners of bed sheets, under the mattress or bed, small boxes, books/bookcases, makeup cases, over-the-counter medicine bottles, and empty candy wrappers.

Be Prepared to Defend Your Decision

If you find drugs or evidence of drug use and confront your child, be prepared to defend your decision. They might try to deflect responsibility by trying to change the subject or shift the blame.

Child: "I can't believe you went through my stuff!? That is such a violation of trust and an invasion of privacy!"

Parent: "I'm sorry you feel that I broke your trust. As a parent, it is my job to keep you safe and healthy. I love you too much to allow something this serious go on. Remember, I asked you on two occasions about this. I need you to tell me the truth so I can understand what's going on. I have no intention of getting mad or punishing you. I want to keep the lines of communication open between us but I need to know if you are in danger."

Question: *How does my drinking affect my children?*

One in five adult Americans grow up with an alcoholic parent. Studies show that children of alcoholics have a greater risk of developing psychological issues and are at a high risk of developing a dependency on alcohol or drugs.

Research has shown that alcoholism runs in families; a child with alcoholic parents is four times as likely to become an alcoholic at some point in life. Verbal and physical abuse as well as neglect is more common in homes with alcoholic parents. A child who grows up with an alcoholic parent might suffer from some of the following issues:

Depression: The child might feel alone and hopeless. Unexpressed and unfelt emotion can lead to a flat internal world or an agitated/anxious defense against feeling internal pain. Anger, rage, and sadness might remain unfelt or unexpressed so there is no resolution. Eventually, these negative feelings can turn inward.

Anxiety: The child might experience free-floating anxiety and worries that appear to have no cause. This might also present as phobias, sleep disturbances, or hypervigilance.

Guilt: The child might believe he or she is the reason for a parent's drinking. They might feel guilty for causing other issues that are going on in the home.

Embarrassment: The child might feel embarrassed about the actions of an alcoholic parent. They might avoid inviting friends to the home or going out in social situations, fearing the parent might be exposed. This can cause isolation and shame.

Anger: The child might feel intense anger toward the alcoholic in the family. He or she might harbor resentments and display negative behaviors due to their anger. In some instances, the non-alcoholic parents might receive more anger from the child.

Confusion: The alcoholic parent might display rapid changes in emotion. They might act differently when they are drinking than when they are not. The child can receive mixed signals and become confused about the relationship with the parents.

Question: *How do I talk to my parents about my addiction and recovery?*

1. **Tell your parents your story.** Explain in a general way how you were first introduced to drugs/alcohol, how experimentation led to dependence, and what you are doing about it now. Use nonjudgmental language so your parents do not become defensive. This might be hard for them to hear. Their first reactions might be fear, disappointment, anger, or misplaced feelings of guilt. Keep in mind, if this is the case, that this is their *first* reaction. Chances are good their feelings will soften over time.

2. **Tell your story to them in stages.** There is no need to share the "gory details" of your addictive behavior—and certainly not when you first begin talking to them about your addiction. When asked questions about your addiction, answer in a general way. You can always add more detail later.

3. **Express your regret for any pain you have caused them.** Try to make amends in ways that are appropriate to your circumstances.

4. **Provide your parents information on addiction and recovery.** You can get such information from your counselor or your support group.

5. **Introduce them to the process of recovery support.** Invite your parents to open meetings and prepare them for what to expect. Remember that it is normal for parents to be somewhat jealous of the benefit you get from professional counselors and from recovery support groups.

6. **Connect your parents with other parents.** Encourage them to attend Al-Anon, Families Anonymous, or Nar-Anon meetings.

7. **Discuss ways your parents can support your recovery.** Some of these might be very simple, such as transportation to counseling or support meetings.

8. **Tell your parents you need to be responsible for your recovery.** Make it clear that their cooperation is welcome but not mandatory, and that this is something they can't do for you.

9. **Negotiate clear expectations.** Let them know what you will do and what they can do to improve future communication and problem solving.

10. **Find support elsewhere.** If your parents aren't yet ready to offer communication and support about your recovery, find others who can offer you guidance and support.

Characteristics of Adult Children of Addiction

1. **Learned helplessness:** People lose the feeling that they can affect or change what's happening to them. They give up and become "helpless," which can also affect other areas of life.

2. **Emotional constriction:** Numbness and shutdown as a defense against overwhelming pain; lack of authentic facial and verbal expressions of emotion.

3. **Distorted reasoning:** Convoluted attempts to make sense and meaning out of a chaotic, confusing, frightening or painful experience that feels senseless. This can take the form of "magical thinking" depending on the age when the child experiences this pain.

4. **Loss of trust and faith:** Due to deep ruptures in primary dependency relationships and the sense of breakdown of an orderly world, the adult child of an alcoholic might have trouble trusting others.

5. **Hypervigilance:** Anxiety, waiting for the other shoe to drop—constantly scanning the environment and relationships for signs of potential danger or repeated rupture.

6. **Traumatic bonding:** An unhealthy bonding style resulting from power imbalance in relationships and lack of other sources of support.

7. **Loss of ability to receive caring and support:** Because of the numbness and shutdown that follow childhood trauma, the adult child might find it difficult or impossible to let others show their love.

8. **Problems with self-regulation:** Problems developing normal and socially acceptable responses in thinking, feeling, and behavior. Thinking might be black and white, either/or. The tendency to go from calmness to rage, without intermediate stages.

CHAPTER 27

Ending the Blame Game

The search for someone or something to blame for the addiction of a loved one is normal, natural, and completely futile. Why some family member become addicts and other family members do not is not fully understood. We do know that there appear to be three major contributing factors.

Genes, Environment, and Development

Genetics. Addiction appears to be triggered by a particular interaction among our genes, environmental influences, and personal development. Research suggests there is a genetic predisposition to addiction. Children of addicts/alcoholics are statistically four times more likely to develop the disease in their lifetime. This research also makes clear that having a genetic predisposition *does not always lead to addiction.*

The role of environment. We have moved past the "nature vs. nurture" regarding addiction. We now think a specific interplay between genetics and the environment (epigenetic) is needed for addiction to develop. Environmental factors can include family, friends, socioeconomic status, and physical location. Peer pressure; physical, emotional, or sexual abuse; trauma, divorce, and financial stresses are also thought to play a role.

Personal development. Finally, personal development appears to contribute to addictive vulnerability. The age, type of drug, frequency of use, and amount/strength of dosage all play a role in addiction. Other factors include personality, psychological make-up, disposition, and attraction to risk-taking behavior.

Intergenerational transmission. In addition to the three major factors, there is research to suggest they can be transmitted from one generation to the next. This phenomenon goes well beyond inheriting similar facial characteristics or body type. It involves distinct aspects of personality, speech patterns, and mental health issues. These characteristic have been known to skip a generation or two and appear in individuals who have never met one another or been alive at the same time.

CHAPTER 28

Creating a Family Genogram

To gain more insight into the way personality, addiction, and mental health characteristics are transmitted between generations, you can create a genogram.

Factoid 💡 **Genogram**

A pictorial display of a person's family relationships. It goes beyond the traditional family tree by including symbols to denote medical, physical, and psychological characteristics. This can be very helpful in recognizing intergenerational behavior patterns.

Benefits of Family Genograms

They provide perspective: Addiction did not just "happen" to show up in your family. Genograms illustrate how influences, characteristics, and behavior patterns pass from one generation to the next.

They promote connection and completeness: There is something profoundly satisfying about seeing how your extended family system works. Learning to see yourself as part of a larger, unfolding pattern opens opportunities for insight, understanding, healing, and compassion.

Exercise: Create a Family Genogram

Here is what you will need:

1. One large piece of paper, ideally 2 x 3 feet. The back side of holiday gift-wrapping paper is good source of paper.
2. A pencil and eraser.
3. Colored markers: blue, red, yellow.
4. An uncluttered space, like a dinner table.
5. One hour of uninterrupted time.

The Basic Blank Genogram for Three Generations

Example # 1

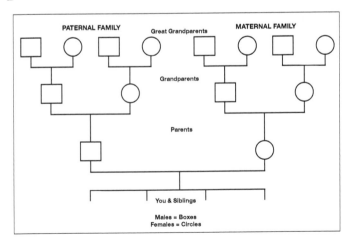

Making a Genogram: Step One

Draw a basic, three-generation genogram. See the legend below to depict different types of marital arrangements.

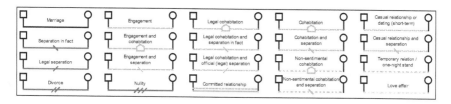

Making a Genogram: Step Two

Add to your genogram any mental health conditions, (depression, anxiety, bipolar disorder, schizophrenia, eating disorders); addictions (drugs, alcohol, gambling, work, sex, pyromania, kleptomania); or criminal activity.

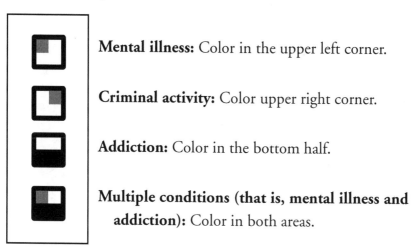

Mental illness: Color in the upper left corner.

Criminal activity: Color upper right corner.

Addiction: Color in the bottom half.

Multiple conditions (that is, mental illness and addiction): Color in both areas.

Example # 2

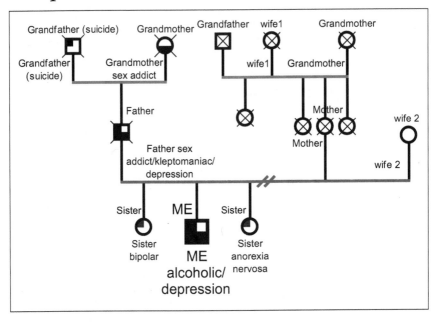

Making a Genogram: Step Three

Add lines to denote emotional relationships among family members. See the legend below for emotional relationship symbols.

Example # 3

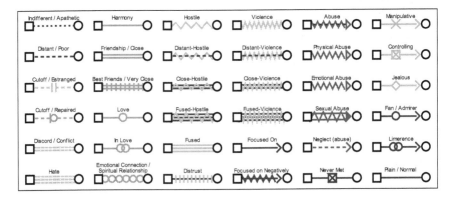

Genogram Pattern Recognition

The paternal and maternal sides of this family's genogram show distinctly different patterns. The paternal side of the genogram displays an intergenerational pattern of suicide, depression, and addiction. Relationships among family members appear distorted by tension, abuse, and abandonment.

The maternal family lineage presents quite differently. There appear to be close, supportive relationships among the generations. There is a distinct absence of tension, abuse, or mental health issues. Finally, there are no mental health or addiction issues present on the maternal side of the genogram.

Example # 4

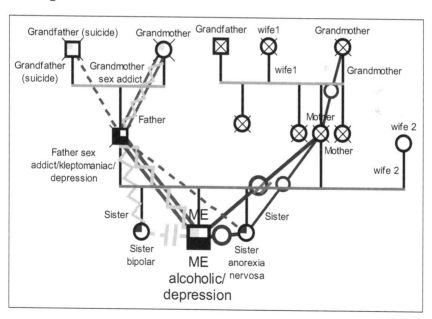

Genogram Reflections

What intergenerational family roles, behavior patterns, relationships, and instances of addictions or mental illnesses did you notice?

_____

_____

_____

_____

_____

Did creating a genogram help you see your family in a new light?

_____

_____

_____

_____

_____

Reflecting on your own family genogram, how do you feel about knowing you are a part of a legacy that stretches back in time? Describe what feelings come up for you during the exercise.

_____

_____

_____

_____

_____

PART SEVEN

Clinician's Guide to Addiction Treatment

Everything You Ever Wanted to Know about Addiction Treatment, But Were Never Taught at School

Chapter 29: Clinical Barriers to Treatment

Chapter 30: Clinical Ambivalence toward AA

Chapter 31: America's Love of "Wonder Drugs"

Chapter 32: Our Confused Drug Policies

Chapter 33: Assessing Your Views on Addiction

Chapter 34: Motivational Interviewing

Chapter 35: Guiding Principles of Motivational Interviewing

Chapter 36: The OARS Technique

Clinical Barriers to Treatment

Treating addiction can be a daunting task. Before getting into the specifics of treatment strategies, I would like to take a moment to point out a number of unique challenges and barriers associated with addiction treatment. They include:

- Clinical bias against the efficacy of talk therapy.
- Clinical ambivalence toward 12-step model.
- America's love of "wonder" drugs.
- Tolerance of recreational drug use.
- "Pressure to prescribe" in the medical community.
- Confused public policy toward drugs.
- Personal history/experience/biases toward addiction.

Negative Bias against Talk Therapy

The mental health field has been slow to acknowledge addiction as a mental disorder. In fact, the American Psychological Association (APA) did not even include addiction (Addictive Use Disorder) as a stand-alone diagnostic category until the *Diagnostic and Statistical Manual of Mental Disorders, 5th Edition* (DSM- 5) was published in 2013.

As a result, clinical education and training for addiction treatment has lagged. A recent look at a number of APA-approved graduate programs (master and doctorate levels) suggests that about 5 percent of total education and training is spent on assessment, diagnosis, and treatment of addiction.

I believe this is might be related to an unspoken bias in the mental health community that psychotherapy is not an effective way to treat addiction. This belief can be traced back to neurologist Sigmund Freud's negative bias on the subject. He asserted that cocaine and opiate addicts were too "resistant" to treat with the "talking method." In fact, after unsuccessfully treating a few patients, Freud turned away or referred those who came to him with addiction issues.

Jung and the Origin
of the Spiritual Solution

Freud referred one of these people to his colleague, Dr. Carl G. Jung. The patient's name was Rowland Hazard. Jung treated him for alcoholism in 1931. We do not know anything about the course of treatment except that Hazard reported his treatment was successful. He returned to the United States confident in his ability to stay sober. A few months later, the patient relapsed. He promptly returned to Jung for an explanation.

The Big Book of AA offers us an account of this encounter:

So he [Rowland H.] returned to this doctor [Jung], whom he admired, and asked him point-blank why he could not recover. He wished above all things to regain self-control. He seemed quite rational and well-balanced with respect to other problems. Yet he had no control whatever over alcohol. Why was this?

He begged the doctor to tell him the whole truth, and he got it. In the doctor's judgment he was utterly hopeless; he could never regain his position in society and he would have to place himself under lock and key, or hire a bodyguard if he expected to live long. That was a great physician's opinion. . . .

The doctor said: "You have the mind of a chronic alcoholic. I have never seen one single case recover, where that state of mind existed to the extent that it does in you." Our friend felt as though the gates of hell had closed on him with a clang.

He said to the doctor, "Is there no exception?"

"Yes," replied the doctor, "there is. Exceptions to cases such as yours have been occurring since early times. Here and there, once in a while, alcoholics have had what are called vital spiritual experiences. To me these occurrences are phenomena. They appear to be in the nature of huge emotional displacements and rearrangements. Ideas, emotions, and attitudes which were once the guiding forces of the lives of these men are suddenly cast to one side, and a completely new set of conceptions and motives begin to dominate them. In fact, I have been trying to produce some such emotional rearrangement within you. With many individuals the methods which I employed are successful, but I have never been successful with an alcoholic of your description."

(From *The Big Book of Alcoholics Anonymous*)

The Big Book goes on to report that Rowland shared this insight with a man named Ebby Thacher, who in turn passed it along to Bill Wilson, the cofounder of AA.

Lost in Translation

Jung's insight into the need for a fundamental psychological paradigm shift revolutionized treatment. He described this mental transformation as a series of sudden, dramatic, "and vital spiritual experiences" that altered the thinking, feeling, behavior, and direction of the addict's life. Jung posited these changes took place below the level of consciousness.

Jung's thinking about the unconscious grew more expansive over time. It came to include the intuitive, instinctual, and archetypal aspects of human experience as well as larger, collective forms, organizing principles, symbols, and images.

Jung did not develop his insights on addiction into a theory or program of interventions. He explains why in a letter he wrote to Bill Wilson in 1961. Jung appears concerned that his highly nuanced ideas about places where spirituality and science appear to rub up against each other—and how to address them in treatment—would be reduced to "misleading platitudes" about the nature of alcoholism.

Quoting from Jung's letter to Wilson:

"These are the reasons why I could not give a full and sufficient explanation to Rowland H., but I am risking it with you because I conclude from your very decent and honest letter that you have acquired a point of view above the misleading platitudes one usually hears about alcoholism.

"You see, alcohol in Latin is *spiritus* and you use the same word for the highest religious experience as well as for the most depraving poison. The helpful formula therefore is: *spiritus contra spiritum.*"

Jung does not elaborate on his three-word, Latin formula in his letter to Wilson or anywhere in his work that I can find. He does, however, link the idea of spirit with an expanded view of Freud's pleasure principle, an animating life force Jung referred to as *Eros.*

"Eros is a questionable fellow and will always remain so . . . He belongs on one side to man's primordial animal nature which will endure as long as man has an animal body. On the other side he is related to the highest forms of the spirit. But he thrives only when spirit and instinct are in right harmony."

(From "The Eros Theory," *Collected Works of C. G. Jung, Volume 7, Two Essays in Analytic Psychology,* 28)

Jung also believed that an innate property of Eros is self-healing. If the obstacles impeding the highest expression of this curative life force were removed, Jung appears to suggest, Eros has the ability to potentiate self-healing. When seen through this lens, Jung might be suggesting that accessing Eros in some "vital" transformative way could spark the direction of this life force from its lowest, poisonous expression (addiction) to its highest, healthiest expression and bring the two into a balanced tension of opposites.

CHAPTER 30

Clinical Ambivalence toward AA

To date, the medical and mental health communities have shown no interest or enthusiasm in developing Jung's ideas on addiction treatment. Fortunately for alcoholic and addicts around the world, Jung's ideas took root and flourished in the minds of Bill Wilson and Dr. Bob Smith, the people who cofounded Alcoholics Anonymous in 1935.

Since that time, Alcoholics Anonymous (AA) has grown into the largest, most effective sober support organization in the world. Standing on the shoulders of earlier, spiritually minded organizations (The Washingtonians and the Oxford Group), AA meetings are now being held in 175 countries around the world. According to AA's General Service Office, more than two million people per year attend AA meetings.

(From the AA.org website)

Why Clinicians Should Learn about AA

For reasons that remain obscure to me, the mental health community's view of AA still appears ambivalent. While some clinicians recognize the vital role 12-step programs play in helping their patients stay sober, many others appear to have little interest in, or understanding of, how AA works.

I can only speculate why this is the case. One reason might be ignorance. Most clinicians never learned about the 12-step model in school. It appears few actually go on to educate themselves about AA on their own. As a result, they do not understand how to integrate attendance at 12-step meetings into their treatment plans and are therefore reluctant to do so.

Another reason for clinical wariness might be a bias against referring treatment modalities not included on the APA list of "evidence-based" practices. Still another reason might have to do with reluctance on the part of clinicians to accept "spiritual" support groups as a part of the "behavioral science" of psychology. Or it might just be that clinicians are somehow put off by non-professional treatment interventions.

Regardless of the reasons, I am convinced this ambivalence must be resolved if we are to improve the level of care we provide this underserved population.

Ignorance and Misinformation

To illustrate why therapists need to learn about the 12-step model, I offer a typical example of clinical ignorance and misinformation that I recently witnessed. I once worked for a dual-diagnosis treatment center. I was part of an eight-person clinical team. Three members of this team (including me) were in recovery and were members of AA.

During a clinical meeting, a therapist reported his client told him he was having a hard time "working on his fourth step." The therapist did not know what this meant and asked the clinical team for an explanation. The room fell silent. Team members exchanged blank stares. After a moment, it became clear that none of the clinicians (except the three in recovery) had any idea what this meant.

I finally broke the silence and recited the fourth step: "Made a searching and fearless moral inventory of ourselves." I explained the arduous nature of this step. Individuals engage in a process wherein they take pen to paper and write down every person, place, thing, or institution toward which they hold a resentment. They also identify "their part" in the resentment and write down the "defect of character" (read "cognitive distortion") behind the resentment.

This kind of soul-searching and honestly "taking stock" was certainly difficult for me at times when I completed my own fourth step. I was fortunate enough to be working with a therapist who understood the process and helped keep me motivated and on-task. I cannot imagine doing this work with a therapist who did not understand what I was going through or how to support me.

Adding misinformation to ignorance, the clinical director errone-ously claimed, "More people go out [lose their sobriety] during their fourth step than on any other step." She went on to say, "I think AA put step four in the *wrong* place. People should not be doing this kind of work until at least step nine or ten." The director was not in recovery herself and clearly had no understanding of the 12-step model. Where she got her information is unknown. What is clear, however is how often ignorance and misinformation about AA are passed along as fact.

There is so much wrong with her statement, it is hard to know where to start. My point here is that most clinicians—*even those working in addiction treatment centers*—are ignorant and/or misinformed about the most effective support fellowship for addiction!

Clinician, Educate Thyself

Learning the 12-steps of AA is not just a good idea, it is sound clinical practice. Returning to the comprehensive NIDA outcome study, "regular attendance at 12-step sober support meetings is one of the strongest indicators of long-term (one year or more) sobriety." Why clinicians would not want to learn how to include this pillar of recovery in their treatment plans remains a mystery to me.

Here Are Some Suggestions

- Read *The Big Book of Alcoholics Anonymous* and *Twelve Steps and Twelve Traditions* (both published by Anonymous Press).

- Attend meetings at five *different* 12-step fellowships (for example, Alcoholics Anonymous, Cocaine Anonymous, Narcotics Anonymous, Sex Addicts Anonymous, Gamblers Anonymous, Overeaters Anonymous, or Debtors Anonymous). All have meetings that are open to the public.

- Attend three different types of meetings. There are a wide variety of meeting formats. I suggest attending a "speaker" meeting, where one individual tells his or her story in detail; a book/12-step study meeting, where program literature is read and discussed; and a meeting at which many individuals share their personal "experience, strength, and hope."

- Connect with AA members who have achieved long-term sobriety and ask about their experience. You might be surprised to find out how many of your colleagues are in recovery.

- Attend five different Al-Anon or Ala-Teen meetings. These fellowships are for the loved ones of addicts and alcoholics in and out of recovery.

- Maintain a current directory of 12-step meetings for interested clients and display 12-step-related pamphlets in your waiting room.

- Maintain 12-step assessments forms (available for free on 12-step websites).

- Get comfortable with 12-step lingo. Appropriate use of phrases, such as *One day at a time; We are only as sick as our secrets; Progress, not perfection;* or *Keeping your side of the street clean* can go a long way to making your client feel understood and supported, as these reflect key concepts in 12-step discussions.

CHAPTER 31

America's Love of "Wonder Drugs"

Amerrica has a long-standing fascination with "wonder drugs"—medications that claim to instantly cure any malady. Pharmaceutical companies and enterprising individuals have been marketing highly addictive "wonder drugs" for more than a hundred years in the United States. The use of children in advertisements for narcotic-laced elixirs speaks volumes about our cultural naiveté regarding these highly addictive substances.

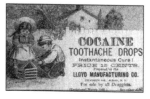 

Our Pill-Popping Culture

The United States consumes 75 percent of all prescription medications in the world. Most of these medications improve the quality and quantity (length) of our lives. But the flood of habit-forming medications also has resulted in many unintended and deadly consequences.

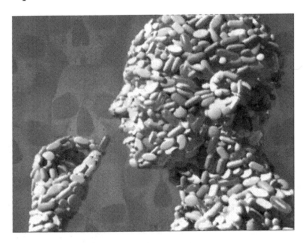

The Explosion of Opiate Addiction

Nora D. Volkow, MD, executive director of NIDA, reports the growth of opiate use in America is "skyrocketing." Dr. Volkow cites three reasons for this alarming increase in opiate addiction:

1. A drastic increase in the number of prescriptions written and dispensed over the last twenty-five years.
2. Greater social acceptability for using medications for purposes other than prescribed.
3. Aggressive marketing by pharmaceutical companies.

The number of opiate prescriptions (for hydrocodone and oxycodone) skyrocketed from 76 million in 1991 to 219 million in 2011 in the United States—a staggering 288 percent increase.

The United States accounts for almost 100 percent of the world's total consumption of hydrocodone (brand name

Vicodin) and 81 percent of the world's consumption of oxycodone (brand name Percocet).

(From the National Institute on Drug Abuse website)

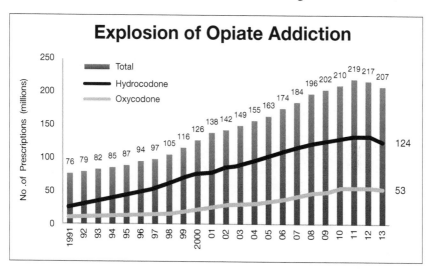

The Pressure to Prescribe

Doctors often feel trapped in a system that punishes them for not writing prescriptions for opiates or other addictive substances when requested by patients.

In a recent (2015) conversation with the head of psychiatry at a large healthcare provider who asked to remain anonymous, I had a chance to learn more about this problem. He explained that a doctor's performance is now evaluated, in large measure, by patient satisfaction. This evaluation plays an important role in the doctor's performance review, compensation, and job security.

"This creates a system in which doctors are reluctant to say no when patients request opiates, stimulants, and sedatives," he said. "Doctors today are in a double bind. Even if they do not believe addictive drugs are indicated for a patient, they are often afraid the patient will complain and give them a poor evaluation if their request is denied."

In today's changing healthcare landscape, physicians often find themselves in an awkward and sometimes adversarial relationship with the individuals in their care. In my view, fear of poor patient evaluations and legal liability have distorted the relationship between healthcare professionals and patients in ways that does a disservice to both.

CHAPTER 32

Our Confused Drug Policies

America's public policy toward drugs has zigzagged for the past century. Periods in which government policy viewed addiction as a mental health issue requiring treatment have been followed by periods in which addiction was viewed as a law enforcement issue requiring punishment.

Here are some selected highlights that illustrate the United States' confused, contradictory public policies toward drugs and addiction.

1914: The Harrison Narcotics Act, the United States' first federal drug policy, becomes law. Manufacture and sale of marijuana, cocaine, heroin, and morphine is restricted. Between 1915 and 1938, more than 5,000 physicians are convicted and fined or jailed for prescribing drugs to addicts on "maintenance" programs (Trebach, 1982).

1919–1933: The National Prohibition Act becomes the 18th Amendment to the US Constitution. Manufacturing, distributing, and consuming alcohol becomes illegal. These laws lacked popular support and are openly flouted. "Prohibition" is repealed by the 21st Amendment to the US Constitution in 1933.

1935: The first federal "narcotics farm" (US Public Health Service Hospital) opens in Lexington, Kentucky, to treat drug addiction. It had only a 7 percent success rate.

1966: President Lyndon Johnson passes the Narcotic Addict Rehabilitation Act, which expands funding for research and programs. Alcoholism and drug addiction are viewed as public health issues requiring treatment, not punishment.

1971: President Richard Nixon declares, "America's public enemy number one in the United States is drug abuse." To defeat this enemy, Nixon declares an all-out "war on drugs." Funding for addiction treatment is slashed; funding for local law enforcement and interdiction is increased.

1981: "Just say No!" is First Lady Nancy Reagan's answer to addiction. This marks the start of a sharp escalation in criminal prosecution of drug addicts. Federal government adopts a "zero tolerance" posture toward drug use and sale. Addiction is now a law enforcement issue and is aggressively prosecuted. Incarceration for nonviolent drug offenses skyrockets 800 percent (from 50,000 cases in 1980 to 400,000 in 1997). The United States now incarcerates a larger percentage of its citizens that any other country in the developed world.

1991: President George H.W. Bush funds "The Decade of the Brain." Research programs find conclusive evidence that substance addiction is a "primary, progressive, and chronic brain disease."

1992: The Substance Abuse and Mental Health Administration (SAMHSA), a federal agency charged with improving the quality and availability of prevention, treatment, and rehabilitative services

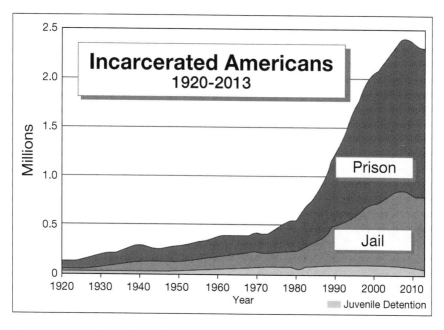

for drug and alcohol addiction, is created. Funding for programs and research recognizing addiction as a disease increases.

2000: President George W. Bush reignites the "war" on drugs. SAMHSA funding is slashed. Local law enforcement agencies (municipal police departments) receive large infusions of funding and paramilitary weaponry. By 2008, more than 40,000 paramilitary-style SWAT raids are conducted on American citizens annually.

2009: President Barack Obama candidly admits marijuana use. SAMHSA funding is increased and the number of nonviolent marijuana arrests is reduced. States begin to decriminalize marijuana use.

CHAPTER 33

Assessing Your Views on Addiction

What do you believe?

Given these confusing cultural signals, it is no wonder most Americans are ambivalent about the use and abuse of drugs. The growing tolerance and decriminalization of some drugs, like marijuana, are increasing right alongside increased prosecution and imprisonment for other drug offenses.

What do you believe? The assessment below is designed to help you clarify your views on drug use, addiction, and treatment. The intention is to identify your growing edges and suggest areas for further study and training. These questions might also shine a light on hidden biases or fears that shape your feelings about how to treat this challenging population.

Do you believe addiction is a disease or a choice?

_____

_____

What is your personal experience with drugs/alcohol use? How have these experiences influenced your view of addiction?

_____

_____

Do you, or your family or friends, have addiction issues?

_____

_____

How comfortable are you working with addicts and alcoholics?

_____

_____

Do you feel sufficiently educated and trained to treat addicts and alcoholics? If not, what is missing?

_____

_____

Do drug addicts and/or alcoholics scare you?

_____

_____

How do you define terms like abstinence, sobriety, and recovery? Is there a difference among them?

_____

_____

What is your understanding of dual diagnosis?

_____

_____

How does dual diagnosis impact treatment, and are you sufficiently trained to treat clients with this diagnosis? If not, what is missing?

_____

_____

What is the role of psychiatry and addiction medicine in treatment?

_____

_____

How familiar are you with motivational interviewing (MI)?

_____

_____

How comfortable are you using MI language and techniques in assessment, diagnosis, planning, treatment, and aftercare planning?

_____

_____

What is Step One of the 12 Steps of AA?

_____

_____

How many AA meetings have you personally attended? What was your experience like?

_____

_____

Are you familiar with Al-Anon? Ala-Teen? Other 12-step fellowships?

_____

_____

How does the 12-step model of recovery work?

_____

_____

How does your client's work in AA affect your relationship with him or her, your treatment planning, or interventions you use in session?

_____

_____

What is your understanding of the role of spirituality in recovery?

_____

_____

Take a moment and reflect on your growing edges. What skills do you need to learn, practice? What countertransference issues need to be monitored, processed, and resolved?

_____

_____

_____

_____

_____

_____

_____

_____

_____

_____

_____

CHAPTER 34

Motivational Interviewing

M otivational interviewing (MI) was originally developed by William R. Miller in the 1980s to help treat alcoholism. He collected his ideas in a book, *Motivational Interviewing: Helping People Change.* Since that time, MI has been continually refined and adapted to help facilitate behavioral change in many areas.

Jassin M. Jouria, MD, describes motivational interviewing this way:

> "Motivational interviewing is a collaborative process that edifies the client and makes him or her responsible for personal choices. It is not necessarily a stand-alone type of therapy, but instead can be incorporated into treatments and routine care for clients with various health issues, including those with physical health problems, mental health issues, or substance abuse and addiction."

> (From *Motivational Interviewing* by Jassin M. Jouria)

Stages of Change

Motivational interviewing divides the process of change into five distinct stages (see chart below). Although the stages are distinct, the process of change is dynamic. Clients often move back and forth between stages, straddle two stages at the same time, or appear to get stuck on a single stage for an extended period of time.

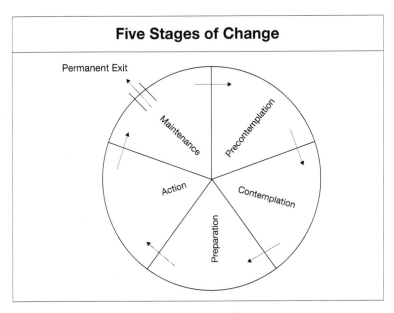

Five Stages of Change

Permanent Exit
Maintenance
Precontemplation
Action
Contemplation
Preparation

Precontemplation

As the name suggest, this refers to a stage in which the clients are not yet aware or open to the need for change, despite feedback from family and friends that they have a problem. Resistance and resentment toward the idea of changing behavior is typical at this stage.

Contemplation

The individual acknowledges the existence of problems associated with using but is not necessarily ready to make any changes.

Preparation/Planning

The person is ready to consider making changes. This stage is often where ambivalences about the need to change are processed and resolved.

Action

Individuals actively engage in the work of change. This is a time of intense energy and activity as they work on changing their thoughts, feelings, and behaviors. The action stage requires sustained energy to continue the process of change despite temporary setbacks or uncomfortable feelings.

Maintenance

This is an ongoing stage in which individuals focus on consolidating the changes into a balanced, sustainable routine.

Meeting Clients Wherever They Are

Motivational interviewing matches interventions with the client's stage of readiness. On the following pages is a chart that matches stages and interventions:

Stage of Change	MI Intervention
Precontemplation	Establish rapport, ask permission, and build trust. Raise doubts or concerns in the client about substance-using patterns by exploring the meaning of events that brought the client to treatment or the results of previous treatments. Elicit the client's perceptions of the problem. Offer factual information about risks of substance use. Provide personalized feedback about assessment findings. Explore pros and cons of substance use. Help a significant other intervene. Examine discrepancies between perceptions of clients and others. Express concern and keep the door open.
Contemplation	Normalize ambivalence. Help the client "tip the decisional balance scales" toward change by eliciting and weighing pros and cons of substance use and change. Changing extrinsic to intrinsic motivation. Examining the client's personal values in relation to change. Emphasizing the client's free choice, responsibility, and self-efficacy for change. Elicit self-motivational statements of intent and commitment from the client. Elicit ideas regarding the client's perceived self-efficacy and expectations regarding treatment. Summarize self-motivational statements.
Preparation/ Planning	Clarify the client's own goals and strategies for change. Offer a menu of options for change or treatment. With permission, offer expertise and advice. Negotiate a change—or treatment—plan and behavior contract. Consider and lower barriers to change. Help the client enlist social support. Explore treatment expectancies and the client's role. Elicit from the client what has worked in the past either for him or others whom he knows. Assist the client to negotiate finances, child care, work, transportation, or other potential barriers. Have the client publicly announce plans to change.

Stage of Change	MI Intervention
Action	Engage client in treatment and reinforce the importance of remaining in recovery. Support a realistic view of change through small steps. Acknowledge client difficulties in early stages of change. Help the client identify high-risk situations through a functional analysis and develop appropriate coping strategies to overcome these. Assist client in finding new reinforcers of positive change. Help client assess strength of family and social support.
Maintenance	Help client identify and sample drug-free sources of pleasure (i.e., new reinforcers). Support lifestyle changes. Affirm the client's resolve and self-efficacy. Help the client practice and use new coping strategies to avoid a return to use. Maintain supportive contact (e.g., explain to the client that you are available to talk between sessions). Develop a "SOBER action plan" if the client resumes substance use. Review long-term goals with the client.

CHAPTER 35

Guiding Principles of Motivational Interviewing

Empathy

*P*eople don't care what you know unless they know that you care. Without empathy, no amount of information, threats, or entreaties will motivate your client to change. Empathy is required for clients to feel they are not alone and that someone actually understands and cares about them.

Empathy creates a therapeutic environment in which the client feels safe to open up. Maintaining an open and nonjudgmental attitude engenders safety and security. This people-centric idea, based on the work of psychologist Carl Rogers holds that genuine warmth and unconditional acceptance toward your client is the foundation of the therapeutic alliance. The clinician meets the client wherever they are.

Discrepancy

Discrepancy refers to the gap between where the client is and where he or she wants to be. Raising discrepancies shines a light on unresolved ambivalences that stand in the way of closing this gap. Clarifying discrepancies empowers clients by giving them the information they need to break down problems into smaller, more manageable tasks.

Raising discrepancies can also be used to increase client self-efficacy by pointing out interim progress toward a goal. "Remember how overwhelmed you got by just thinking about picking up the phone and calling your parents? Today, you call them three or four times a week without giving it a second thought."

Four Ways of Rolling with Resistance

Clinicians frequently encounter resistance from clients. It is important to recognize that resistance is a normal and necessary part of the client's struggle to resolve ambivalences. The fear and frustration about change is often externalized by the client and projected onto the clinician.

1. **Shift the focus.** There might be times when clients project their fear of rejection or failure onto the clinician by pushing back or attempting to blame and shame them. Rather than rebut the resistance, try shifting the focus to another part of the issue on which you both agree.

   Client: "Why are you pushing me to get a job? It is easy for you to sit back and tell me what to do. You do not have a record. You don't have to work for minimum wage."

Clinician: "I hear you. I get you do not think it is realistic for you to get a job right now. What I am focusing on is collecting your work experience into a résumé to identify your skills, strengths, and preferences."

2. **Agree with a twist.** This technique enables you to continue in a positive flow by agreeing with the client and adding a slight twist to keep things on track.

Client: "You and my husband are on my back about my drinking. You should walk a mile in my shoes. My husband is no picnic. You would drink if you had to put up with him day in and day out."

Clinician: "You are right. I do not know what it is like living with your husband. In fact, there is a lot I do not know about your situation. Thanks for reminding me that this problem is bigger than blaming one person. Drinking problems involve the whole family."

3. **Reframe.** Reflecting back your client's issue from a different, more positive perspective can often shift his or her feelings about the matter and help them move on. Reframing "acknowledges the validity of the client's raw observations, but offers a new meaning . . . for them" (Miller and Rollnick, *Motivational Interviewing: Preparing People to Change Addictive Behavior,* 1991, 107).

Client: "My parents constantly nag me about smoking pot. They call me a stoner and say I am wasting my talent or not living up to my potential. It hurts my feelings and makes me mad."

Clinician: "What I hear is your folks recognize how talented you are and are trying to motivate you, even though they are not going about it in a nice or positive way."

4. **Siding with the negative:** This paradoxical technique can be quite effective. The idea is to play devil's advocate by siding with the negative aspect of your client's ambivalence to amplify the discrepancy so the client gets to experience their ambivalence in a different way.

> **Client:** "I know my family thinks I'm a boozer. It might even be affecting my health. But that doesn't make me a broken-down alcoholic or that I have to go someplace to dry out and quit forever."

> **Clinician:** "Your position on your drinking is fairly clear. You do not really think it is a problem and, even if it is, you do not feel ready to change right now. My sense is, if you are happy with your drinking and the direction your life is headed, making changes would be too hard for you. I wonder whether you think you are capable of changing, if you found out drinking was damaging your relationships, health, and career."

Promoting Self-Efficacy

Many clients have lost faith in their ability to stay sober. They no longer believe they can make or maintain behavioral change. To help promote change in this area, clinicians can model this behavior for clients by recognizing a client's strengths and expressing belief in the client. Instilling this belief in your clients is essential if they are going to develop the resilience needed to overcome temporary setbacks without spiraling back into addiction.

Self-efficacy describes the client's self-confidence in his or her ability to perform in a specific area of their life. Clients can have a high level of self-efficacy in one area and a low level in another. For example, a client can have a great deal of self-efficacy when it comes to business or athletics but very little about staying sober.

Self-efficacy is a crucial ingredient in the formula for change, but it must be met with an equally high commitment to doing the ongoing work of recovery.

The OARS Technique

MI developed a mnemonic of helpful therapeutic techniques:
OARS
- Open-ended questions (OEQ)
- Affirmations
- Reflective statements
- Summarize

Open-Ended Questions

These are questions that cannot be answered with a yes or a no. Closed-ended questions tend to stop conversations and might feel intrusive or judgmental. OEQs tend to open conversations and are judgment neutral. They show respect and empower clients to answer in any way they want.

Affirmations

The use of affirmations in a clinical setting is different from the sobriety Skill #2 described in Chapter 5 on "Cognitive-Based Sobriety

Skills." Instead of positive, recovery-centric statements to shift from addictive to sobriety-based thinking, the therapeutic use of affirmations by the clinician is used to strengthen the therapeutic alliance and promote client self-efficacy. Well-constructed, MI affirmations are specific, emotionally charged, positive, in the present tense, and concise.

Closed-ended questions	Open-ended questions
Did you get your hair cut?	*Tell me about your trip to the barber.*
Are you feeling depressed?	*What is going on inside you right now?*
Have you found a job?	*What's new with the job search?*
Are you still sober?	*How are you doing with your sobriety plan?*

Open-Ended Question Exercise

Turn these closed-ended questions into open-ended questions.

Closed-ended questions	Open-ended questions
Are you doing your morning sobriety tasks?	
Do you get triggered at work, school, home?	
Are you getting along better with your parents?	
Did you get the items on your to-do list done?	
Are you still arguing with your partner?	

Be Authentic

The most important thing about using affirmations is to be sincere. The words you use and the way you say them are certainly important. If your client senses you are being inauthentic, patronizing, or otherwise insincere, your affirmations will likely have the opposite effect. Remember, addicts are highly sensitive to criticism, dishonesty, manipulation, and plain old BS. When you use affirmations, make them authentic.

"Wow, sounds like you really handled that situation well. Thank you for telling me."

"I know you worked hard to make this happen. I am proud to witness you accomplishing this goal."

"Not everyone is willing to admit they need help. I admire your courage."

"This is a tough subject to talk about. Bringing it up yourself says a lot about your character and desire to work on your issues."

"I feel for you. Who likes to try something new and come up short? I sure do not. It takes guts to change old habits. I admire your courage. Frankly, you did not miss by much!"

Reflective Listening and Statements

Reflective listening and responses are good ways of building empathy. It requires us to actively listen and reflect back what we think is going on. For example, if your client states he is mad at his parents for telling him to get help or get out of the house, you might reflect,

"It sounds like you feel your parents are pushing you into treatment."

This validates the client's feelings and builds empathy by demonstrating that you understand how he feels.

Reflective listening/commenting empowers the part of the client that is open to change. This is done in a positive way, reframing ambivalence.

"What I also hear is that, even if you were open to the idea of change, you don't like feeling pressured or being given ultimatums."

In both cases, you are signaling you understand what your client is thinking and feeling. When you demonstrate empathy in this way, you strengthen the therapeutic alliance while keeping open the door to change.

Reflective Comment Starters

Here are some generic ways to start a reflective comment.

- "It sounds like . . ."
- "What I hear you saying . . ."
- "So, on the one hand it sounds like . . . and yet, on the other hand . . ."
- "It seems as if . . ."
- "I get the sense that . . ."
- "It feels as though . . ."
- "Let me see if I understand what you are saying . . ."
- "I get the feeling you . . ."

Reflective Phrases

- "It sounds like you are becoming more concerned about your . . ."
- "It sounds like there was a time when your (negative behavior) was a good way to (avoid a problem). But today it appears to create more problems than it solves."
- "I am getting the feeling you want to change, but you still have concerns about (doubt, fear, problem)."
- "Correct me if I am wrong, but what I hear is that (addictive use/behavior) is not a problem you feel you need to solve right now, but you are willing to look at some time in the future."

- "I get the feeling there is a lot of pressure on you to change, and you are not sure you can do it because of difficulties you had when you tried in the past."

The Columbo Approach

The Columbo approach refers to the behavior of a TV detective played by Peter Falk in the 1970s series, *Columbo*. This character had a low-key, disarming way of interrogating suspects. He would ask an open-ended question and listen intently to the person's answer. He would then appear to reflect on the answer for a moment and feign puzzlement about a discrepancy between the person's last statement and something he or she had said previously.

Columbo would do this by asking a question, thinking about the answer, and then asking a follow-up question to help him better understand the situation. These questions were asked in friendly, nonconfrontational, and nonjudgmental ways. It was more like Columbo was confused and needed the individual's help to clarify an apparent contradiction.

In MI terms, Columbo was heightening discrepancies between what clients say they want and the way they behave without evoking defensiveness or resistance. When done skillfully, this technique can uncover client ambivalences and support the part of the client that wants to change.

Examples of Columbo Approach

"Please help me clear this up. You said earlier that your drinking is not interfering with your career or family life. That it is all under control. Now I'm hearing that you partied last weekend and missed work on Monday and that your wife and boss are both mad at you. I'm wondering if one had anything to do with the other."

"So, let me see if I have this right. You want to save up so you can move to a better school district for your kids. You told your wife this is your top priority. Then last week you spent your paycheck on cocaine and now you have to borrow money just to pay the rent. How does that get you any closer to your goal of moving to a better place?"

"What I am hearing is that your kids are everything to you and that you are worried about keeping custody of them. You also told me that child services makes home visits and performs drug screenings on a random basis. You just mentioned you smoke crack with your boyfriend a couple of times a week when he stops by your house. I am wondering how this behavior might affect your keeping custody of your children."

Providing Summaries

Summaries are a special form of reflection that therapists can use to recap part or all of a session. Summaries communicate that you are paying attention and understand your client. They are also an opportunity to highlight parts of the session in which the client expressed willingness to change or demonstrated self-efficacy.

Summaries also can function as a way to point out discrepancies, work through ambivalences, and strengthen/support those parts of the client that are open to change. Finally, summaries can highlight ongoing progress and bolster your client's spirits after they have suffered a temporary setback.

Example # 1

"What I heard today is concern on your part about your drinking; the amount of money you are spending, the DUI arrest. You also demonstrated insight. You acknowledged that not drinking will impact all areas of your life; who you hang out with and what you do with your time. You are smart enough to know this is an important and somewhat difficult decision."

Example # 2

"Over the past couple of weeks you have been talking about the pros and cons about using opiates. My sense is you have been weighing your options and that recently you seem to have noticed there are more pros than cons about getting clean. Another factor that has tipped the scales in favor of getting sober is your wife's decision to move out until you get your life back on track. When you put these together, it is easy to see why you are leaning in the direction of getting sober and staying sober."

Example # 3

"I hear that you feel like nothing is changing and that you feel stuck. When you look back to the start of our time together, your cravings were so bad that you had to stay in bed the entire day. You hated your job and saw no way out. Now you have a much better job, a clean track record, and you are on your way back to school. Overall, it looks like you have made plenty of strides."

Building a Robust Referral Network

The multidimensional disease of addiction requires a multidimensional network of referral resources for proper treatment. Instead of locating referrals resources on an "as-needed" basis, I suggest you be proactive and start building your network right away.

Building this referral network will give you an opportunity to connect with other addiction-savvy individuals and become part of that community. My experience in this area is that the more time I spend cultivating this network, the more I improve as a clinician and the more referrals from others I receive.

Here is a list of referral resources to include in your network. I suggest you identify two of each: a primary resource and a backup in the event the other is not available.

- Addiction-savvy primary care physicians and specialists (liver, heart, lungs, kidneys)
- Addiction-savvy psychiatrists
- Detox facilities
- Local IOP (intensive outpatient) treatment programs
- Local and remote residential (inpatient) treatment programs
- Dual-diagnosis treatment centers
- Specialized dual-diagnosis treatment centers for eating disorders, sex or gambling addiction, or severe mental health diagnoses
- Nurse practitioners/occupational therapists
- Dieticians/nutritionists
- Acupuncturists/massage therapists
- Physical therapists/personal trainers
- Addiction-savvy family and criminal attorneys
- Addiction-savvy accountant
- Up-to-date meeting directories to local 12-step fellowships

The Road Ahead

We are losing our loved ones to the disease of addiction at an alarming rate. Every day more than 120 of our sons and daughters, spouses or partners, brothers and sisters, mothers and fathers, aunts and uncles, friends and loved ones die from their addiction to drugs and alcohol. In the words of Nora Volkow, executive director of NIDA, we are in the throes of a "public health epidemic with devastating consequences." This crisis must not go unmet.

The Staying Sober Handbook is a resource specifically designed to meet this crisis head-on in three important ways.

- First, to treat those suffering from addiction with the best evidence-based treatment protocols.
- Next, teach families, friends, and loved ones how to begin healing themselves, families, and relationships.
- Finally, provide mental health professionals with the special education and training they desperately need to effectively treat the disease of addiction.

You Can Make a Difference

If you share my passion to confront this crisis with treatment, education, understanding, and action, here are steps you can take.

- **Give addicts and loved ones a copy of this book.** This is a direct way to take positive action rather than reminding these individuals what they already know—they have a problem.

- **Send me the names of organizations in your** community where I can give educational talks about staying sober. These include municipal agencies, civic organizations, schools, clubs; any setting you believe my message needs to be heard.

- **Give addicts, friends, families, and loved ones my contact information.** Tell them effective treatment is available and that I stand ready to help.

howard@stayingsoberhandbook.com

www.stayingsoberhandbook.com

My Promise to You

On the first page of this book, I made you a promise—if you were *ready*, I would take you through *The Staying Sober Handbook* and teach you how to maintain long-term sobriety health and wellness. I told you that recovery is an ongoing process and that I would be there to help and support you at every bend in the road.

I am renewing that promise to you on this last page. I want to continue to walk the path of recovery with you on the road ahead. Please contact me. Let me know how I can support you in your recovery today and tomorrow. Sign up for my newsletter at info@ stayingsoberhandbook.com.

Let me know how you are doing. Email me with questions, comments, or if you need local referrals and resources. Contact me with feedback about this book or other recovery-related topics about which you want to learn. Most of all, contact me if you are struggling and need help. My mission is to meet you wherever you are and provide help, not judgment. Contact me at: howard@stayingsoberhandbook.com

Special Offer

Finally, I have a special offer for those who want to share the gift of sobriety, health, and wellness with others. I am offering a 10 percent discount to those who purchase three or more copies of *The Staying Sober Handbook*. To take advantage of this offer, please contact me directly at: howard@stayingsoberhandbook.com or call at 424-781-7949.

Thank you for giving me the opportunity to be of service. I look forward to seeing you on the road ahead.

Love,

Howard

12-Step and Self-Help Groups

Note: Website and phone numbers
were accurate at time of printing.

Adult Children of Alcoholics (ACA) http://www.adultchildren.
org/ 310.534.1815

Al-Anon Family Groups http://www.al-anon.org/ 818.760.7122
(LA) 888.4AL.ANON

Alcoholics Anonymous (AA) http://www.aa.org/ 323.936.4343 (LA
Central Office) 215.870.3400

Anorexia Nervosa and Associated Disorders http://www.anad.org/
310.463.5106 (LA) 847.831.3438

Co-Anon (Cocaine Addicts) Family Groups http://www.co-anon.
org/ 520.513.5088

Cocaine Anonymous (CA) http://www.ca.org/ 310.216.4444 (LA
Hotline) 800.347.8998

Co-Dependents Anonymous (CoDA) http://coda.org 323.969.4995

Co-Dependents of Sex Addicts (COSA) http://www.cosa-recovery.
org/ 763.537.6904

Compulsive Eaters Anonymous-HOW http://www.ceahow.org/ 562.942.8161

Crystal Meth Anonymous (CMA) http://www.crystalmeth.org/ 213.488.4455

Debtors Anonymous (DA) http://www.debtorsanonymous.org/ 310.822.7250 (LA) 781.453.2743

Gam-Anon (Gambler's Anonymous) http://www.gam-anon.org/ 818.377.5144 (LA Hotline) 718.352.1671

Gamblers Anonymous (GA) http://www.gamblersanonymous.org/ 877.423.6752 (SoCal Hotline) 213.386.8789

Marijuana Anonymous (MA) http://www.marijuana-anonymous. org/ 818.759.9194 (LA County) 800.766.6779

Nar-Anon (Narcotics Anonymous) Family Groups http://www. nar-anon.org/ 310.547.5800 (SoCal) 800.477.6291

Narcotics Anonymous (NA) http://www.na.org/ 818.773.9999

Nicotine Anonymous (NICA) http://www.nicotine-anonymous. org/ 800.642.0666 (SoCal) 414.750.0328

Overeaters Anonymous (OA) http://www.oa.org/ 505.891.2664

Recovering Couples Anonymous (RCA) http://www.recovering-couples.org/ 510.663.2312

S-Anon http://www.sanon.org/ 818.973.2235 (LA) 800.210.8141

Sex Addicts Anonymous (SAA) http://www.sexaa.org/ 213.896.2964 (LA) 800.477.8191

Sex and Love Addicts Anonymous (SLAA) http://www.slaafws.org/ 323.957.4881 (LA) 210.828.7900

Sexaholics Anonymous (SA) http://www.sa.org/ 213.480.1096 (LA) 866.424.8777

Sexual Compulsives Anonymous (SCA) http://www.sca-recovery. org 800.977.HEAL

Workaholics Anonymous (WA) http://www.workaholics-anonymous.org 510.273.9253

Mental Health

Authentic Recovery Center (ARC) http://www.arctreatment.com/ (LA) 877.415.HOPE (4673)

The Bridge to Recovery (Bowling Green, Kentucky) http://www.thebridgetorecovery.com/ **877.866.8661**

Clearview Treatment Programs http://www.clearviewtreatment.com/ (LA) 310.446.0110 ext. 100

Cottonwood Centers (Tucson, Arizona) https://www.cottonwooddetucson.com/ 800.877.4520

Emotions Anonymous (EA) http://www.emotionsanonymous.org/ 651.647.9712

InsightLA https://www.insightla.org/ 310.774.3325

KeyStone Center (Chester, Pennsylvania) http://www.keystonecenterecu.net/ 800.733.6840

Life Adjustment Team http://lifeadjustmentteam.com/ 310.572.7000

The Meadows (Wickenburg, Arizona) http://www.themeadows.org/ **800.510.5572**

Milestones Ranch Malibu http://www.milestonesranch.com/ 310.456.9190

Prominence Treatment Center http://www.prominencetreatment.com 877.383.2284

Recovery, Inc. http://www.recovery-inc.org/ 310.306.6766

Sierra Tucson (Tucson, Arizona) http://sierratucson.crchealth.com/ 800.842.4487

Soba Recovery Center http://www.sobamalibu.com 866.447.5298

Visions Adolescent Treatment Centers http://www.visionsteen.com/ (Malibu) 818.889.3665

Addiction Resources

Allies in Recovery (AiR) http://alliesinrecovery.net/ 413.210.3724

The Bodin Group http://www.thebodingroup.com/ 310.806.9655 (LA) 800.874.2124

Gentle Path Press gentlepath.com 800.708.1796

Hired Power Recovery Assistant Program http://www.hiredpower. com/ 800.910.9299

Recovery Coaches International recoverycoaching.org

SHARE! Self-Help and Recovery Exchange http://www.shareselfhelp. org/ 310.305.8878

Spirit Recovery http://www.spiritrecovery.com/ 310.455.0810

Recovery Resources
for Young People

Beautiful Boy: A Father's Journey through His Son's Addiction by David Sheff

The Big Book Unplugged: A Young Person's Guide to Alcoholics Anonymous by Anonymous

Clean: A New Generation in Recovery by Chris Beckman

Daughter's Drug Addiction by Trina Hayes

Just Love Her: A Mother's Journey of Healing through Her Leaving Dirty Jersey: A Crystal Meth Memoir by James Salant

Lost and Found by Christy Crandell

The Lost Years: Surviving a Mother and Daughter's Worst Nightmare by Kristina Wandsilak and Constance Curry

Nice Girls Don't Drink by Sarah Hafner

Teenage Addicts Can Recovery by Shelly Marshall

Tweak: Growing up on Methamphetamines by Nic Sheff

Young Sober and Free by Shelly Marshal

Bibliography

Anonymous: *Alcoholics Anonymous, The story of how many thousands of men and women have recovered from alcoholism.* New York City, Alcoholics Anonymous World Services Inc., 1939.

Anonymous: *Twelve Steps and Twelve Traditions.* New York City, Alcoholics Anonymous World Services Inc., 1952.

Beatty, Melody: *Codependent No More: How to stop controlling others and start caring for yourself.* Center City, Minnesota, Hazelden, 1986.

Beck, Aaron T. and Arthur Freedman and associates: *Cognitive Therapy of Personality Disorders.* New York, Guilford Press, 1990.

Becker, Ernest: *The Denial of Death.* New York, First Free Press, 1973.

Begley, Sharon: *Train your Mind, change your Brain: How a new science reveals our extraordinary potential to transform ourselves.* New York, Ballantine Books, 2007.

Bennett-Goleman, Tara: *Emotional Alchemy: How the mind can heal the heart.* New York, Three Rivers Press, 2001.

Bolen, Jean Shinoda: *Goddesses in Everywoman: A new psychology of women.* New York, Harper & Row, 1984.

Bolen, Jean Shinoda: *Gods in Everyman: A new psychology of men.* New York, Harper & Row, 1989.

Bourne, Edmund J.: *The Anxiety and Phobia Workbook.* Oakland, California, New Harbinger Publications, 2005.

Brach, Tara: Radical Acceptance: *Embracing your life with the heart of the Buddha.* New York, Bantam Books, 2003.

Brown, Brené: *Daring Greatly: How the courage to be vulnerable transforms the way we live, love, parent, and lead. New* York, Gotham Books, 2012.

Burns, David D.: *The Feeling Good Handbook.* New York, Penguin Putnam, 1999.

Campbell, Joseph: *The Hero with a Thousand Faces.* New York, Bollingen Foundation, 1949.

Carnes, Patrick: *Out of the Shadows: Understanding sexual addiction.* Minneapolis, Minnesota, CompCare Publications, 1983.

Center for Substance Abuse Treatment. *Clinical Supervision and Professional Development of the Substance Abuse Counselor.* Treatment Improvement Protocol (TIP) Series 52. DHHS Publication No. (SMA) 09-4435. Rockville, Maryland, Substance Abuse and Mental Health Services Administration, 2009.

Center for Substance Abuse Treatment. *Detoxification and Substance Abuse Treatment Training. Enhancing Motivation for Change in Substance Abuse Treatment.* Treatment Improvement Protocol (TIP) Series, No. 35.HHS Publication No. (SMA) 13-4212. Rockville, Maryland, Substance Abuse and Mental Health Services Administration, 1999.

Center for Substance Abuse Treatment. *Substance Abuse: Clinical Issues in Intensive Outpatient Treatment.* Treatment Improvement Protocol (TIP) Series 47. DHHS, Publication No. (SMA)

06-4182. Rockville, Maryland, Substance Abuse and Mental Health Services Administration, 2006.

Doidge, Norman: *The Brain that Changes Itself: Stories of personal triumph from the frontiers of brain science.* New York, Viking Penguin, 2007.

Frankl, Viktor E.: *Man's Search for Meaning: An introduction to logotherapy.* New York, Touchstone, 1959.

Freud, Sigmund: *Introductory Lectures on Psycho-Analysis.* New York, W.W. Norton & Company, 1966.

Freud, Sigmund: *On Dreams.* New York, W.W. Norton & Company, 1952.

Germer, Christopher K. and Ronald D. Siegel, Paul R. Fulton, eds.: *Mindfulness in Psychotherapy.* New York, Guilford Press, 2005.

Glasser, William: *Take Charge of Your Life: How to get what you need with choice theory psychology.* Bloomington, Indiana, iUniverse, 2011.

Gordon, James, S.: *Unstuck: Your guide to the seven-stage journey out of depression.* New York, Penguin Press, 2008.

Gorski, Terence T. and Merlene Miller.: *Staying Sober: A guide for Relapse Prevention.* Independence, Missouri, Herald House/ Independence Press, 1986.

Gorski, Terence T.: *Passages through Recovery: An action plan for preventing relapse.* Center City, Minnesota, Hazelden, 1989.

Gorski, Terence T.: *The Staying Sober Workbook: A serious solution for the problem of relapse.* Independence, Missouri, Herald House/ Independence Press, 1992.

Haroutunian, Harry: *Being Sober: A step-by-step guide to getting to, getting through, and living in recovery.* New York, Rodale Books, 2013.

Herman, Judith Lewis: *Trauma and Recovery: The aftermath of violence—from domestic abuse to political terror.* New York, Basic Books, 1992.

James, John W. and Russell Friedman: *The Grief Recovery Handbook: An action program for moving beyond death, divorce and other losses including health, career, and faith.* (20th anniversary expanded edition) New York, Harper Collins, 2009.

Jung, C.G.: *The Archetypes and the Collective Unconscious.* Collected Works, v. 9, 1, Princeton University Press, 1956.

Jung, C.G.: *Two Essays on Analytical Psychology.* Collected Works, v. 7, Princeton University Press, 1956.

Jung, C.G.: *Memories, Dreams, Reflections.* New York, Vintage Books, 1961.

Jung, C.G.: *Symbols of Transformation.* Collected Works, v. 5, Princeton University Press, 1956.

Kabat-Zinn, Jon: *Coming to our Senses: Healing ourselves and the world through mindfulness.* New York, Hyperion, 2005.

Kabat-Zinn, Jon: *Full Catastrophe Living: Using the wisdom of your body and mind to face stress, pain, and illness.* New York, Bantam Dell, 2005.

Kelly, John F. and William L. White, eds.: *Addiction Recovery Management: Theory, research, and practice.* Springer, New York, Humana Press, 2011.

Kindlon, Dan and Michael Thompson: *Raising Cain: Protecting the emotional life of boys.* New York, Ballantine Books, 2000.

Kornfield, Jack. *A Path with Heart: A guide through the perils and promises of spiritual life.* New York: Bantam Books, 1993.

Kornfield, Jack: *The Wise Heart: A guide to the universal teachings of Buddhist Psychology.* New York: Bantam Books, 2008.

Levine, Peter A.: *Healing Trauma*. Boulder, Colorado, Sounds True, 2008.

Meade, Michael J.: *The World Behind the World: Living at the ends of times*. Seattle, Washington, Greenfire Press, 2008.

Miller, Alice: *The Drama of the Gifted Child: The search for the true self*. New York, Basic Books, 1997.

Napier, Augustus Y. and Carl Whitaker: *The Family Crucible: The intense experience of family therapy*. New York, HarperCollins, 1978.

Nhất Hạnh, Thich: *The Miracle of Mindfulness*. Boston, Massachusetts, Beacon Press, 1976.

Newberg, Andrew and Mark Robert Waldman: *How God Changes your Brain: Breakthrough Findings from a leading neuroscientist*. New York, Ballantine Books, 2009.

O'Neil, Mike and Charles E. Newbold Jr.: *Boundary Power: How I treat you, how I let you treat me, how I treat myself*. Nashville, Tennessee, Sonlight Publishing, 1994.

Ogden, Pat: *Trauma and the Body: A sensorimotor approach to psychotherapy*. New York, W.W. Norton & Company, 2006.

Real, Terrance: *I Don't Want to Talk About it; Overcoming the secret legacy of male depression*. New York, Scribner, 1997.

Rosellini, Gayle and Mark Worden: *Of Course You're Angry: A guide to dealing with the emotions of substance abuse*. Center City, Minnesota, Hazelden, 1985.

Ruiz, Miguel Angel: *The Four Agreements: A Toltec wisdom book*. San Rafael, California, Amber-Allen Publishing, 1997.

Sandoz, Jeff: *Alcoholic Iliad/Recovery Odyssey: Utilizing myth as addiction metaphors in family therapy*. Boca Raton, Florida, Brown Walker Press, 2009.

Schoen, David E.: *The War of the Gods in Addiction: C.G. Jung, Alcoholics Anonymous, and Archetypal Evil.* New Orleans, Louisiana, Spring Journal Books, 2009.

Schore, Allen N.: Affect Regulation and the Repair of the Self. New York, W.W. Norton & Company, 2003.

Schwartz, Richard C.: *Internal Family Systems Therapy.* New York, The Guilford Press, 1995.

Siegel, Daniel J.: *The Mindful Brain: Reflection and attunement in the cultivation of well-being.* New York, W.W. Norton & Company, 2007.

Stutz, Phil and Barry Michels: *The Tools: Transform your problems into courage, confidence, and creativity.* New York, Spiegel & Grau, 2012.

Substance Abuse and Mental Health Services Administration, *National Survey of Substance Abuse Treatment Services (N-SSATS): 2011. Data on Substance Abuse Treatment Facilities.* BHSIS Series S-64, HHS Publication No. (SMA) 12-4730. Rockville, Maryland: Substance Abuse and Mental. 2011.

Substance Abuse and Mental Health Services Administration. *Detoxification and Substance Abuse Treatment.* Treatment Improvement Protocol (TIP) Series, No. 45. HHS Publication No.(SMA) 134131. Rockville, Maryland: Substance Abuse and Mental Health Services Administration, 2006.

Substance Abuse and Mental Health Services Administration. *Substance Abuse Treatment for Persons with Co-occurring Disorders.* Treatment Improvement Protocol (TIP) Series, No. 42. HHS Publication No.(SMA) 1 3992. Rockville, Maryland: Substance Abuse and Mental Health Services Administration, 2005.

Teresi, Louis and Harry Haroutunian: *Hijacking the Brain: How drugs and alcohol addiction hijacks our brains the science behind twelve-step recovery.* Bloomington, Indiana, Authorhouse, LLC, 2011.

Tolle, Eckhart: *The Power of Now: A guide to spiritual enlightenment.* Novato, California, New World Library, 1999.

White, William L. *Slaying the Dragon: The history of addiction treatment and recovery in America.* Bloomington, Illinois, Chestnut Health Systems/Lighthouse Institute, 1998.

Williams, Rebecca E. and Julie S. Kraft: *The Mindfulness Workbook for Addiction: A guide to coping with the grief, stress, and anger that trigger addictive behaviors.* Oakland, California, New Harbinger Publications, 2012.

Yalom, Irvin D., *The Theory and Practice of Group Therapy.* New York, Basic Books, 1995.

Index

Note: Page numbers followed by *f* indicate figures.

AA. *See* Alcoholics Anonymous
Abundance, affirmations about, 50
Action
  contrary (*See* Contrary actions)
  in PRINT process, 111, 193–194
  as stage of change, 269, 271f
Action plan, SOBER, 119–122
  for boundary setting, 218–219
  description of steps in, 119–122
  for self-defeating behavior
    patterns, 165
Activating events, in cognitive
    behavioral therapy, 34–35
Active listening, 102–105
  vs. bad communication habits, 104
  practice exercise on, 104–105
  skills promoting, 103
Activities, sobriety-centric, 93–123
  active listening, 102–105
  assertive communication, 105–108
  bookending, 115–116
  contrary actions, 116–119
  dealing with resentments, 109–111

Activities, sobriety-centric *(cont.)*
  fun, 99–102
  making amends, 111–114
  SOBER action plan, 119–123
  support group meetings, 93–98
  therapy, 98–99
  in width of sobriety, 128–130
Addict role in families, 199
Addiction
  as chronic medical condition, 13,
    17–19, 20f
  contributing factors in, 233–234
  cycle of, 13, 17, 21–29, 22f, 29f,
    122, 123f, 167f
  desire to be "normal" in, 17–18
  "disease" model of, 13
  impact on brain, 10
  impact on families, 198–199
  management of, 13, 17
  negative consequences of, 25–27
  negative core beliefs in, 45–46
  recovery from (*See* Recovery)

Addiction *(cont.)*
  self-assessment of views on,
    263–266
  treatment of (*See* Treatment)
Addiction medicine, 10
Adrenalin, 24
Advice, giving, 104
Affirmations, 44–50
  authenticity in, 280–281
  core beliefs of addicts and, 45–46
  in daily schedule, 139
  definition of, 44
  in OARS technique, 279–281
  practice exercises on, 48–50
  repetition of, 45
  tips for optimizing, 46–47
Aggressive communication, 105
Alcohol abuse
  impact on brain, 188–189
  impact on nutrition, 88–89
  public policy and, 259–260
  searching for evidence of, 226–227
  signs of, 225–226
Alcohol paraphernalia, getting rid of,
    80
Alcoholics Anonymous (AA), 93–98
  bookending in, 115
  clinical ambivalence toward,
    249–253
  fun activities in, 100
  history of, 93
  meetings of, 96–97
  on nature of alcoholism, 188–189
  spirituality in, 94–95, 244–247
  sponsors in, 95, 97–98
  12 steps of, 95–96, 251–252
Allen, James, *As a Man Thinketh*, 44
All-or-nothing thinking, 35
Amends, making, 111–114
  vs. apologies, 111–112

Amends, making *(cont.)*
  practice exercise on, 114
  steps in, 111–112
  tips on, 112–113
American Psychological Association
    (APA), 243–244, 250
Anger, in children of alcoholics, 228
Anhedonia, 100
Anxiety, among children of
    alcoholics, 228
Anxiety-based self-defeating behavior
    patterns, 159–161
APA. *See* American Psychological
    Association
Apologies, vs. making amends,
    111–112
As a Man Thinketh (Allen), 44
Assertive communication, 105–108
  vs. aggressive and passive
    communication, 105–106
  examples of, 106–107
  practice exercise on, 107–108
  tips on, 107
Authenticity, in affirmations, 280–281
Automatic thoughts, in CBT mood
    logs, 40f, 41–42, 43f

Balance, in Mid Recovery, 141–142
Beck, Arnold, 34
Behavior(s), sobriety-centric, 77–123
  boundary setting, 77–79
  healthy diet and nutrition, 87–91
  personal appearance/hygiene, 82–84
  self-soothing, 84–87
  sober home/work/school
    environments, 79–82
  in width of sobriety, 128–130
Behavioral signs of alcohol or drug
    abuse, 225–226

Behavioral therapy. *See* Cognitive behavioral therapy
Beliefs. *See also* Religious beliefs
in CBT mood logs, 40f, 41–42, 43f
core, 45–46, 47f
irrational, 34–35
negative self-, 23, 45–46
self-limiting, 192
Bias, against talk therapy, 243–244
The Big Book of Alcoholics Anonymous, 27, 73, 94, 115, 188, 244–245
Biochemicals, 189
Blame
for addiction, 18, 37, 233
in bad communication, 104
Body
impact of stress on, 22, 23
mapping triggers in, 67–69
Bonding, traumatic, in adult children of addiction, 231
Bookending, 115–116
Boundaries
defending, 219–220
practice exercise on, 219–220
role of, 215
setting, 77–79, 215–220
types of, 215–218
Brain
healing process in, 141
impact of addiction on, 10
impact of drugs and alcohol on, 25, 28, 188–189
impact of prayer on, 70–71
Breathing
in mindfulness, 34, 59–61, 110
in SOBER action plan, 120–121, 165, 218
Buddha, 57–58, 153
Buddhism, 57–58

Burns, David D., *The Feeling Good Handbook,* 37
Bush, George H. W., 260
Bush, George W., 261

Careers, impact of addiction on, 25–26
Caretaker/Rescuers, 164
Carnes, Patrick, 45
CBT. *See* Cognitive behavioral therapy
Centers for Disease Control (CDC), 25, 198–199
Challenges in recovery, 157–194
incomplete recovery, 169–177
post-acute withdrawal symptoms, 179–194
self-defeating behavior patterns, 159–167
Change(s)
promises to, 27–28
stages of, 268–269, 268f, 270f–271f
to thinking (*See* Cognitive behavioral therapy)
Checklists
for negative consequences of addiction, 26
for personal appearance and hygiene, 83–84
for Spectrum of Sobriety, 14, 133f, 135–136, 136f
Chief Enablers, 199
Children, impact of parents' drinking on, 228–229, 230–231
Choice, problems with concept of addiction as, 18–19
Chronic medical condition, addiction as, 13, 17–19, 20f
Circles of sobriety, 78–79, 80–81

Clark, Kenneth, 148
Clothing, 82–83
Clown/Jokesters, 160–161
Clumsiness, as post-acute withdrawal
  symptom, 181
Codependence, 205–213
  vs. enabling behavior, 205
  long-term problems with, 206
  recovering from, 211–213
  self-assessment of, 207–209
  short-term benefits of, 205–206
Cognitive behavioral therapy (CBT),
  33–43
  ABCs of, 35, 35f
  cognitive distortions in, 34–43
  mood logs in, 39–43, 40f, 42f
  origins of, 34
  principles of, 34–35
Cognitive distortions
  definition of, 34
  examples of, 37–39
  in mood logs, 39–43, 40f, 42f
  types of, 35–37
Cognitive post-acute withdrawal
  symptoms, 180, 183
Cognitive skills, 33–56
  affirmations, 44–50
  cognitive behavioral therapy, 33–43
  gratitude, 50–52
  journaling, 54–56
  meditation, 52–53
  overview of, 33
Collapse
  post-acute withdrawal symptoms
    in, 188
  in Spectrum of Sobriety, 132
Columbo approach, 283–284
Communication
  active listening in, 102–105
  aggressive, 105

Communication (cont.)
  assertive, 105–108
  bad habits in, 104, 105–106
  forms of, 102, 103f
  passive, 106
  passive/aggressive, 106
Compliant/Invisible/Conformist
  individuals, 162
Conclusions, jumping to, 36
Conformist/Compliant/Invisible
  individuals, 162
Confusion, in children of
  alcoholics, 229
Consciousness, 64
Consequences
  of addiction, types of, 25–27
  in cognitive behavioral therapy, 35
Contemplation stage of change,
  268, 270f
Contrary actions, 116–119
  breaking cycle of addiction with,
    28–29
  creating list of, 117–119, 122
  examples of, 117–118, 121
  facing fears through, 116–117
  practice exercise on, 118–119
  in SOBER action plan, 121–122,
    165, 218–219
Control
  external loss of, 188
  internal loss of, 185–186
Core beliefs
  negative, 45–46
  positive, 46, 47f
Crecelius, Ruth Hock, 74
Cynics, 162

Daily gratitude list, 51–52, 115, 139
Daily meditation, 52–53

Daily schedules, 137–142, 138f, 140f
Deaths, addiction-related, 25, 287
Decision making
  impact of drug use on, 25
  in post-acute withdrawal
    symptoms, 180
Decriminalization, of marijuana, 261
Delayed gratification, 141
Denial
  dealing with resentments
    through, 110
  family healing after end of,
    200–201
Dependency-based self-defeating
  behavior patterns, 163–164
Depression, among children of
  alcoholics, 228
Depression-based self-defeating
  behavior patterns, 162–163
Depth of recovery, 145, 147–149, 148f
Detaching with love, 212–213
*Diagnostic and Statistical Manual of
  Mental Disorders* (DSM), 244
Diaphragmatic breathing, 59, 110,
  120–121
Diet, 87–91, 139
Diminishing returns, law of,
  22–23, 23f
Discrepancies, in motivational
  interviewing, 274
"Disease" model of addiction,
  problems with, 13
Distorted reasoning, in adult children
  of addiction, 230
Dopamine, 25, 99–100
Drug(s), pharmaceutical
  in addiction treatment, 99
  Americans' use of, 255–258
  public policy on, 259–261

Drug abuse
  impact on brain, 25, 28, 188–189
  as moral failing vs. medical
    condition, 19
  searching for evidence of, 226–227
  signs of, 225–226
Drug paraphernalia, getting rid of, 80
"Dry drunk" syndrome, 128–129
DSM. *See Diagnostic and Statistical
  Manual of Mental Disorders*

Early Recovery, 31–123
  breaking cycle of addiction in,
    28, 122
  cognitive skills in, 33–56
  focus of, 12, 15–16
  mindfulness skills in, 57–75
  sobriety-centric behaviors in,
    77–123
Education
  of clinicians, 252–253
  on codependency, 213
  in family healing, 203, 213
  impact of addiction on, 25–26
Embarrassment, in children of
  alcoholics, 228
Emotion(s)
  in adult children of addiction, 230
  cognitive distortion of, 36
  cognitive skills in shaping of, 33
  in cycle of addiction, 27–28
  mindfulness and, 61–62
  recovering capacity for, 67
  stress and, 23–24
Emotional boundaries, 216
Emotional constriction, in adult
  children of addiction, 230
Emotional dysregulation, as post-
  acute withdrawal symptom, 180

Emotional flatness, as post-acute
  withdrawal symptom, 186
Emotional post-acute withdrawal
  symptoms, 180–181, 183,
  185–188
Emotional reasoning, 36, 41
Emotional self-soothing, 86
Emotional Volcanoes, 161
Empathy
  in communication, 103
  in motivational interviewing, 273
  in OARS technique, 281–282
Empowerment, personal, 14
Enabling behavior
  vs. codependence, 205
  in families, 199, 203–204
Environmental factors, in addiction,
  233–234
Eros, 247
Euphoric recall, 24
Exercise, physical, 85, 100
External loss of control, 188

Failure to Launch individuals, 163
Falk, Peter, 283
Families, 195–240
  as addicted systems, 197–201
  boundary setting in, 215–220
  children of addiction in, 228–229,
    230–231
  codependence in, 205–213
  denial in, 200–201
  genograms of, 235–240
  impact of addiction on, 198–199
  promoting healing in, 203–204
  roles in, 199–200
  rules and meetings in, 221–222
  safety issues in, 222–230

Families (cont.)
  setting boundaries in, 215–220
  treatment for all members of, 204
Family manager role, 199
Family meetings, 221–222
Family safety plan, 222–224
Fears
  childhood, 191–192
  facing, 116–117, 191–192
Feeling, recovering capacity for, 67.
  See also Emotion
The Feeling Good Handbook (Burns), 37
Finances, impact of addiction on,
  25–26
Financial boundaries, 217–218
fMRI (functional Magnetic
  Resonance Imaging), 10
Forgiveness, asking, vs. making
  amends, 111–112
Fortune-telling, 36, 41
The Four Agreements (Ruiz), 44
Francis, Pope, 153
Francis of Assisi, Saint, 74–75
Freud, Sigmund, 244, 247
Frost, Robert, 83
Fun, in sobriety, 99–102
Functional Magnetic Resonance
  Imaging (fMRI), 10

Gandhi, Mahatma, 153
Gastrointestinal system, 88
Generations, transmission of
  addiction across, 234
Genetics, of addiction, 233
Genograms, family, 235–240
  benefits of, 235–236
  definition of, 235
  examples of, 236f, 238f, 239f
  how to make, 236–238

Genograms, family (cont.)
  recognizing patterns in, 239
  reflections on, 240
Gibran, Kahlil, 153
Giving, counterintuitive nature of, 151–152
The Godfather (movie), 67
Gorski, Terence, 179, 181
Gratification, delayed, 141
Gratitude, 50–52
  benefits of, 50
  in daily schedule, 139
  writing daily list of, 51–52, 115, 139
Group therapy, 98
Growth, in Long-Term Recovery, 145
Guilt
  in children of alcoholics, 228
  in cycle of addiction, 27–28
Gums, damage to, 90

Habit, developing sobriety as, 140–141
Harrison Narcotics Act, 259
Hazard, Rowland, 94–95, 244–246
Health. *See* Mental health; Physical health
Helplessness, learned, 230
Hero role in families, 199
Higher Power (HP)
  definition and use of term, 71
  developing partnership with, 72
Hobbies, rediscovering old, 100–101
Home, creating sober environment at, 79–82
House rules, 221–222
How God Changes Your Brain (Newberg and Waldman), 70–71

HP. *See* Higher Power
Hydrocodone, 256–257
Hygiene, 82–84, 139
Hypervigilance, in adult children of addiction, 231

"I" statements, 106–108
Impaired coordination, as post-acute withdrawal symptom, 181
Impaired thinking, as post-acute withdrawal symptom, 180
Incarceration rates, 260, 261f
Incomplete recovery, 169–177
  post-acute withdrawal symptoms in, 170, 174, 176
  stages of, 171–176, 172f
Individual therapy, 98–99
Inner circle of sobriety, 78–79
Interests, rediscovering old, 100–101
Intergenerational transmission of addiction, 234
Internal loss of control, 185–186
Interviewing, motivational. *See* Motivational interviewing
Inventory, of negative consequences of addiction, 26
Investigating alternatives, in PRINT process, 111, 193–194
Invisible/Conformist/Compliant individuals, 162
Irrational beliefs, in cognitive behavioral therapy, 34–35
Is AA For You? (pamphlet), 94

Johnson, Lyndon, 260
Jokester/Clowns, 160–161
Jokester/Mascots, 200
Jouria, Jassin M., 267

Journaling, 54–56
  benefits of, 54–55
  tips for, 55–56
Judge/Perfectionists, 161
Judgmental remarks, 104
Jung, Carl Gustav, 244–247
  capacity for joy, 101
  on denial, 110
  and spirituality in AA, 94–95,
    244–247
  on treatment of addiction, 94–95,
    244–247, 249
  on the unconscious, 246

Labeling, 36–37
Lapse, in Spectrum of Sobriety, 132
Learned helplessness, 230
Legal status, damage to, 26
Legislation, on drugs, 259–260
Listening
  active, 102–105
  reflective, 281–284
Liver damage, 89
Long-Term Recovery, 143–155
  acts of service in, 151–155
  focus of, 12, 16
  maintenance and growth in, 145
Lost Child role, 199
Love, detaching with, 212–213
Lung capacity, 59–60

Magnification, 36
Maintenance
  in Long-Term Recovery, 145
  in Spectrum of Sobriety, 132
  as stage of change, 269, 271f
Marijuana
  adverse effects of using, 89–90
  decriminalization of, 261

Mascot/Jokesters, 200
Meade, Michael, *The World Behind the World*, 116
Medical care, 99
Medical model of addiction, 13, 17–20
Medications. *See* Drug(s)
Medicine, addiction, 10
Meditation
  mindfulness, 34, 57–64
  reading daily, 52–53, 139
  sample, 53
Meetings, family, 221–222. *See also* Alcoholics Anonymous; Support group meetings
Memory
  in euphoric recall, 24
  problems with, as post-acute withdrawal symptom, 180
Mental filters, 35
Mental health problems
  addiction-related, 26–27
  nutrition and, 91
Mental self-soothing, 86
Metabolism, impact of addiction on, 88
MI. *See* Motivational interviewing
Mid Recovery, 125–142
  daily schedule in, 137–142, 138f, 140f
  focus of, 12, 16
  Spectrum of Sobriety in, 131–136
  width of recovery in, 127–130
Midbrain, 25, 28
Middle circle of sobriety, 78–79, 81
Miller, William R., 267
Mind reading, 36, 41
Mindfulness, 57–75
  benefits of, 58–59
  breathing in, 34, 59–61, 110

Mindfulness (cont.)
in Buddhism, 57–58
in daily schedule, 139
in dealing with resentments, 110
definition of, 34, 57
goal of, 57
with post-acute withdrawal
symptoms, 189
practice exercise on, 62–64
role in sobriety, 61–62
in SOBER action plan,
120–121, 165
Mindfulness skills, 57–75
mapping triggers, 67–69
meditation, 57–64
overview of, 34
prayer, 70–75
visualization, 64–65
Mirroring, 103
Mislabeling, 36–37
Mixed/dependency-based
self-defeating behavior patterns,
163–164
Mood logs, in cognitive behavioral
therapy, 39–43, 40f, 42f
Mood signals, biochemical, 189
Moral failing, perception of addiction
as, 18–19
Motivational interviewing (MI),
267–277
principles of, 273–277
stages of change in, 268–269, 268f,
270f–271f
"Must" statements, 36

Narcotic Addict Rehabilitation
Act, 260
Nasal breathing, 60–61

National Council on Alcoholism and
Drug Dependence, 226
National Institute on Drug Abuse
(NIDA), 19, 180, 181, 252,
256–257
National Institutes of Health (NIH),
87–88, 91
Negative consequences of addiction
checklist of, 26
types of, 25–27
Negative core beliefs, of addicts, 45–46
Negative emotions
cognitive distortion of, 36
mindfulness and, 61–62
stress in, 23–24
Negative experiences
in CBT mood logs, 40f, 41–42, 43f
overgeneralization of, 35
Network
referral, 285–286
sober support, 98–99, 122
Neurochemistry
of addiction, 10
of drug use, 25
New beliefs, in CBT mood logs, 40f,
41–42, 43f
New fun activities, 101–102
Newberg, Andrew, How God Changes
Your Brain, 70–71
Next steps, in PRINT process, 111,
193–194
NIDA. See National Institute on
Drug Abuse
Niebuhr, Karl Paul Reinhold, 74
NIH. See National Institutes of
Health
Nixon, Richard, 260
Non-verbal communication, 102,
103, 103f
"Normal," desire to be, 17–18

Nostalgia, in euphoric recall, 24
Nutrition, 87–91, 139

OARS technique, 279–285
　affirmations in, 279–281
　Columbo approach and, 283–284
　open-ended questions in, 279, 280f
　reflective statements in, 281–284
　summaries in, 284–285
Obama, Barack, 261
Observation, in SOBER action plan,
　120, 165, 218
Old beliefs, in CBT mood logs, 40f,
　41–42, 43f
Open-ended questions
　in Columbo approach, 283–284
　in good communication, 103
　in OARS technique, 279, 280f
Opiates
　impact on nutrition, 88
　rise in addiction to, 256–257, 257f
Organ damage, 89
"Ought" statements, 36
Outer circle of sobriety, 78–79, 80–81
Overgeneralization, 35, 41
Oxycodone, 256–257

Pancreas, damage to, 89
Paraphernalia
　getting rid of, 80
　searching for, 226–227
Para-verbal communication, 102, 103f
Parents
　alcoholism of, impact on children,
　　228–229, 230–231
　talking about addiction with,
　　229–230
Partnership, with Higher Power, 72
Passive communication, 106

Passive/aggressive communication, 106
PAWS. *See* Post-acute withdrawal
　symptoms
PAWS PRINT, 193–194
Perception, cognitive skills in
　restructuring of, 33
Perfectionist/Judges, 161
Performance, stress and, 22–23
Personal appearance, 82–84
Personal development, as contributing
　factor in addiction, 234
Personal empowerment, 14
Personality traits
　codependence as, 205
　positive, 48, 49f
　transformation of, 147
Personalization, 37
PET scans, 10
Pharmaceutical drugs. *See* Drug(s),
　pharmaceutical
Physical boundaries, 216
Physical effects of stress, 22, 23
Physical exercise, 85, 100
Physical health problems
　nutrition and, 87–91
　stress-related, 22
　types of addiction-related, 25
Physical post-acute withdrawal
　symptoms, 181, 182
Physical self-soothing, 85–86
Physical signs of drug abuse, 225
Planner, daily, 137–142, 138f
Planning stage of change, 269, 270f
Pleasure centers of brain, 25, 28
Positive core beliefs, 46, 47f
Positive experiences, discounting
　of, 35–36
Positive personality traits, 48, 49f
Positron-Emission Tomography
　(PET) scans, 10

Post-acute withdrawal symptoms
 (PAWS), 179–194
  characteristics of, 180, 181
  definition of, 24, 179–180
  in incomplete recovery, 170,
   174, 176
  major types of, 180–181
  mild, 182–184, 190f
  moderate, 184–187, 190f
  overcoming with PRINTS,
   191–194
  and relapse, 181, 182f, 188
  severe, 187–190, 190f
Prayer, 70–75
  changing approach to, 71–72
  dealing with resentments
   through, 110
  examples of, 72–75
  impact on brain, 70–71
  types of, 70
Precontemplation stage of change,
  268, 270f
Prefrontal cortex, 25, 28
Preparation/planning stage of change,
  269, 270f
Prince/Princesses, 164
PRINT solution
  description of steps in, 110–111
  overcoming PAWS with, 191–194
Privacy issues, in families, 226–227
Problem solving, through
   journaling, 54
Prohibition era, 259–260
Psychiatrists, 99
Psychological signs of alcohol or drug
   abuse, 226
Public policy, on drugs, 259–261
Purge, in PRINT process, 111,
  193–194

Questions, open-ended, 103, 279,
  280f, 283–284
Qur'an, 153

Rational response, in CBT mood logs,
  40f, 41–42, 43f
Reading
  of daily meditation, 52–53
  mind, 36, 41
Reality check, in PRINT process,
  111, 193–194
Reasoning
  distorted, 230
  emotional, 36, 41
Rebel/Scapegoats, 159–160, 199
Reconnecting, in SOBER action
  plan, 122
Recovery
  challenges in (See Challenges)
  from codependence, 211–213
  depth of, 145, 147–149, 148f
  length/duration of, 127–128, 128f
  in Spectrum of Sobriety, 132
  stages of, 12, 15–16, 15f (See also
   specific stages)
  width of, 127–130, 128f
Recovery management, 11, 13
Referral network, 285–286
Reflective listening and statements, in
  OARS technique, 281–284
Reframing, in motivational
  interviewing, 275–276
Regression, as stage of incompletion,
  171, 172f, 174–176
Relapse
  and post-acute withdrawal
   symptoms, 181, 182f, 188
  rates of, in addiction vs. other
   chronic conditions, 19, 20f

Relapse (cont.)
  in Spectrum of Sobriety, 132
  as stage of incompletion, 171,
    172f, 176
Relational boundaries, 215–216
Relationships. *See also* Families
  boundary setting in, 77–79, 215–220
  codependence in, 205–213
  damage to, 25
Religious beliefs
  in Alcoholics Anonymous, 94–95
  impact on brain, 70–71
Repetition
  of affirmations, 45
  in stages of incompletion, 171,
    172f, 173–174
Rescuer/Caretakers, 164
Resentments
  dealing with, 109–111
  definition of, 109
  misconceptions about, 109–110
Resistance, in motivational
    interviewing, 274–276
Revised beliefs, in CBT mood logs,
    40f, 41–42, 43f
Rogers, Carl, 273
Roommates, sober, 80–82
Ruiz, Don Miguel, *The Four
    Agreements*, 44
Rules, house, 221–222

Safety issues, family, 222–230
Safety plan, family, 222–224
  definition of, 222
  guidelines for, 222–223
  sample of, 223–224
SAMHSA. *See* Substance Abuse
    and Mental Health Services
    Administration

Scapegoat/Rebels, 159–160, 199
Schedules, daily, 137–142, 138f, 140f
School. *See also* Education
  creating sober environment at,
    81–82
  impact of addiction at, 25–26
SDBPs. *See* Self-defeating behavior
    patterns
Self-assessment
  of codependence, 207–209
  of views on addiction, 263–266
Self-beliefs, negative, 23, 45–46
Self-blame, 37
Self-care, 84–87
Self-defeating behavior patterns
    (SDBPs), 159–167
  anxiety-based, 159–161
  cycle of, 164–165, 166f
  definition of, 160
  depression-based, 162–163
  mixed/dependency-based, 163–164
Self-destructive behavior, in cognitive
    behavioral therapy, 34–35
Self-efficacy, in motivational
    interviewing, 276–277
Selfishness, end of, 152–153
Self-limiting beliefs, 192
Self-regulation problems, in adult
    children of addiction, 231
Self-sabotage, 175–176
Self-soothing behaviors, 84–87
  definition of, 84
  importance of developing, 84–85
  practice exercise on, 86–87
  types of, 85–86
Serenity Prayer, 73–74, 139
Service, acts of, 151–155
Seventh Step Prayer, 73
Sexual boundaries, 217

Shame
  in bad communication, 104
  in cycle of addiction, 27–28
Shaw, George Bernard, 53
"Should" statements, 36
Sleep problems, as post-acute
  withdrawal symptom, 181
Slip, in Spectrum of Sobriety, 132
SMART plans, 194
Smith, Bob, 94, 249
SOBER action plan, 119–122
  for boundary setting, 218–219
  description of steps in, 119–122
  for self-defeating behavior
    patterns, 165
Sobriety
  circles of, 78–79, 80–81
  cycle of, 29, 29f, 122, 123f, 167f
  depth of, 145, 147–149, 148f
  length/duration of, 127–128, 128f
  Spectrum of, 131–136
  width of, 127–130, 128f
Sobriety activities. See Activities,
  sobriety-centric
Sobriety behaviors. See Behavior(s),
  sobriety-centric
Sobriety skills. See Cognitive skills;
  Mindfulness skills
Spectrum of Sobriety (SOS),
  131–136, 131f
  checklist of, 14, 133f,
    135–136, 136f
  levels of, 131–132
Spiritual boundaries, 216–217
Spiritual damage, 27
Spiritual self-care, 86
Spirituality
  in acts of service, 153
  in Alcoholics Anonymous, 94–95,
    244–247

Sponsors, in Alcoholics Anonymous,
  95, 97–98
Staying Sober approach
  effectiveness of, 11–12
  principles of, 13–16
  stages of, 15–16 (See also specific
    stages)
  timeline with, 12
Stimulants, impact on nutrition, 90
Stress
  in cycle of addiction, 21–24, 28
  definition of, 21
  good vs. bad, 21–22
  hypersensitivity to, as post-acute
    withdrawal symptom, 181
  journaling to reduce, 54
Substance Abuse and Mental Health
  Services Administration
  (SAMHSA), 11, 198, 260–261
Summaries, in OARS technique,
  284–285
Support group meetings, 93–98. See
  also Alcoholics Anonymous
  challenges of attending, 169–171
  clinicians' lack of understanding of,
    250–253
  for codependency, 213
  types of, 93–94
Support network, 98–99, 122

Talk therapy, negative bias against,
  243–244
Talmud, 153
Teeth, damage to, 90
Thacher, Ebby, 246
Therapy, 98–99
  for family members, 204, 213
  ignorance about AA in, 250–252

Therapy *(cont.)*
  motivational interviewing in,
    267–277
  negative bias against, 243–244
  OARS technique in, 279–285
  referral network in, 285–286
  role of, 98–99
  tips for selecting therapist, 98
  types of, 98
Thiamine deficiency, 88
Thinking
  all-or-nothing, 35
  automatic, 40f, 41–42, 43f
  changes to (*See* Cognitive
    behavioral therapy)
  impaired, 180
Third Step Prayer, 72–73
Tidal breathing, 59
Time, vs. width, of sobriety,
    127–128, 128f
Tolstoy, Leo, 197
Trance state
  in cycle of addiction, 24, 28
  definition of, 24
  how to avoid, 28
Transformation, in depth of recovery,
    147–149
Traumatic bonding, in adult children
    of addiction, 231
Treatment, addiction, 241–286.
    See also Therapy
  for all family members, 204
  clinical barriers to, 243–253
  developmental model of, 14, 15
  Jung on, 94–95, 244–247, 249
  motivational interviewing in,
    267–277
  psychiatric drugs in, 99
  public policy and, 259–261
  recent developments in, 10–11

Treatment, addiction (cont.)
  referral network in, 285–286
  "wonder" drugs and, 255–258
Triggers, 67–69
  identifying and mapping, 67–69
  SOBER action plan for, 119–123
Trust, loss of, in adult children of
    addiction, 231
Tunnel vision, 184
12-step model of recovery, 93–96. *See
    also* Alcoholics Anonymous

Unconscious mind
  definition of, 64
  Jung on, 246
  post-acute withdrawal symptoms
    in, 176, 181
  resentments in, 110
  visualization and, 64

Validating phrases, 103
Verbal communication, 102, 103f
Victim role, 163
Visualization, 64–66
  power of, 64–65
  practice exercise on, 65–66
Volkow, Nora D., 256, 287

Waldman, Mark Robert, *How God
    Changes Your Brain,* 70–71
"War on drugs," 260–261
Weekly performance, tracking,
    135–136, 136f
Weekly schedules, 137, 140, 142
Wernicke-Korsakoff syndrome, 88
Width of sobriety, 127–130, 128f
Will power, perception of addiction as
    matter of, 18–19

Wilson, Bill, 18, 74, 94, 246–247, 249
Withdrawal symptoms, acute,
    179–180. *See also* Post-acute
    withdrawal symptoms
"Wonder drugs," 255–258
Work
    creating sober environment at,
      81–82
    impact of addiction on, 25–26

The World Behind the World
    (Meade), 116
Worldview, transformation of, 147
Writing
    daily gratitude list, 51–52, 115, 139
    in journal, 54–56

Zero tolerance policies, 260

howardpgoodman.com